A Black Man Has 9 Lives

Joe McClain Jr.

This is a work of fiction. Names, characters, places and incidents are either the product of the authors imagination or are used fictitiously. Any resemblance to actual events or locales or persons, living or dead is entirely coincidental. From The Mind Of Joe McClain Jr.

DEDICATION

This book is dedicated to the families and memories of Tamir Rice, Trayvon Martin, Freddie Gray, Oscar Grant, Sean Bell, Eric Garner, LaQuan McDonald and everyone who has lost a loved one to the ills of police brutality.

CONTENTS

ACKNOWLEDGMENTS

I thank God, my wife, the people of my hometown (East Chicago, Indiana), the people of my adopted hometown (San Diego, CA) and all who have supported myself and the entire Uprock Publications family.

1 THE FIRST STEP

Transformation is sometimes restoration
it can be disguised in aluminum foil as a wrapped up food
plate
only to be open and find that no food is available to eat
but in the midst of emptiness, a man can sometimes become
full
full of life, full of renewal, full of consequence in the present
tense
all because you made it through your past tense
and tension arises, but so does the sun, and it shines bright
reproducing life through its light
so tell me, what exactly is transformation
is it the making of a new man
or just the bettering of the man that you already were

"It's simple Mrs. Kraylin. The pyramids were a spiritual haven and a way to the afterlife." I just snickered and shook my head.

"You wrong man like usual." The entire class was now

locked in on me. I didn't claim to know everything. When it came to history, however, I didn't mess around. I was sharper than a bulls horn up a Spanish man's ass with information.

"So, Mr. Philosophical. Mr. I'm such a history buff. Enlighten me?" I swear on everything I love, Chris Ferrington was a highly privileged brat who swore everything that came out of his mouth was fact. When in truth, everything that came out of his mouth was pure trash. I guess that was part of being born with a silver spoon in your mouth, 'cause not everyone's parents would buy them a Bentley Coup at 16.

'"Well," as I leaned in from my chair. "The structures are actually diamond shaped. They are built with the same specs above ground as they are underground. Each end is topped off with quartz. You know the ends. The bottom of the diamond and the top of the diamond. Anywho, the moonlight refracted off of the quartz on both ends and gave the illusion of the entire land around the pyramids being illuminated. Therefore, that might be, rather I guarantee that's the reason you see the All Seeing Eye on your dollar bill. They can yell all about how it's God's eye looking over the land or whatever stupid phrase they wanna use. That's all fine and dandy. If you wanna believe that fable, that's ya business. But, that's where the term comes from. If you pull a dollar out, rather, you look at one on a computer seeing how you are a spoiled lil brat, you'll see the illumination around the eye. Now, Mr. Know it all. Tell me, where is the only place on the human body you find quartz at?"

He was stunned silent, as was the whole class. Our teacher Mrs. Kraylin was even locked in behind her desk. I ensured to make eye contact with every one of these people in class so they could feel my emotion without a single word spoken. I once again locked eyes with Chris.

"Well, Mr. Spoiled? Are you gonna answer my question or just sit there with a dumb founded look on that ugly face of yours?"

"Enlighten me," he said so sarcastically. Ahh, how I loved pissin' people like him off.

"Your eyes. You know that organ which you have four of." The class erupted into laughter as the bell rang. We all got up, gathering our things, about to head to the cafeteria for lunch, or wherever we were going.

"Ramses?"

"Yes Mrs. Kraylin? What is it you need?" She walked over to the door and shut it. I figured my ass was in trouble for the remarks I made about Chris. I truthfully didn't care, however, because I couldn't stand him.

"All I want is five minutes of your time, maybe less and the answer to one question. You are very direct and precise with everything in this class. Don't get me wrong. This is a group discussion class, and the whole point is to debate and find a logical solution to the problems that we are trying to solve. However, with you, I see this aura around you when you speak. It's like you command the attention of everyone when you talk. What I really want to know is this. What makes you value history in general more than anything else that we talk about in here?" I smiled at her as I grabbed my backpack and hoisted it over my shoulder.

"Because ma'am. Once you almost become history, you figure out how to appreciate it." With a stunned look on her face, I simply smiled.

"Good day Mrs. Kraylin. Is there anything else that you would like to know?" She simply smiled at me.

"No Ramses. You have a great day yourself." I walked out of her class and down the hall to the doors leading to the stairs. As I pressed the door, I paused for a minute, thinking about the day where I almost became history.

"A lil nigga? Go get me another beer?" There I was, six years old, stuck with my no good Uncle Ronnie. He wasn't worth a damn, but the state of Oklahoma somehow saw me fit to stay with him after my parents both died in a car accident. We lived in Hugo, a little city about 15 minutes from the Texas border. It wasn't much here. Hell, come to think about it, the biggest thing there is Walmart. About four to five thousand people made up this quaint little town. It was a long ways away from the hustle and bustle of Oklahoma City, where I was at all of my life until I got put here with him. I got Unc his beer and brought it back to the table where he and his friends from 'cross the border were playing a game of tunk.

"You'z a good lil nigga man." The table burst out into laughter. Me, I didn't find anything funny at all. Hell, I remembered being called that plenty of times in my young life by groups of drunken hillbillies driving up the road. **"NIGGER BOY!"** seemed to be their favorite quote. I may have not known a lot at my young age, but I did know that word wasn't meant for any good towards me. Even if history shows that it didn't start off like that. I went back to sit in the living room and watch TV while they continued on with their ignorance for the night. Really, I wasn't watching TV. I had a children's book in my hand that was about the Bible. I was scared that I may be whooped if Unc saw me reading, so I had the TV blaring so that he wouldn't assume anything out of the ordinary.

The door was now shut to his room as they wasted the night away smokin' and drinkin'. Life was what it was for me. I was just happy to have a roof over my head, even if it wasn't the greatest roof to live under. I continued to read with Tom and Jerry blaring in the background, turning the TV up louder and louder as they got louder and louder in the nearby room. This continued on for most of the night. Finally, I heard a commotion unlike any other that night, followed by something falling hard on the floor. I didn't know what was going on. I slid back on the couch with hands over my ears. The door flung open as every man ran out besides my uncle. Things got real quiet. Tom and Jerry was now nonexistent to me right now. After about five minutes, I got up to peek in my uncle's room. I saw him on the floor, white foam coming from his mouth, but I didn't know what the hell was going on.

"Uncle Ronnie?" No answer. "Uncle Ronnie?" Again, no answer. I walked in the room and stared at him. He was shaking harder than a possum that had to cross through fox country to freedom. I didn't want to touch him. It was a scary sight. I analyzed him for a good minute to see that there was something sticking out of his arm. A band had been wrapped around the top of his right arm and his shaking spats were now violent as ever. I turned around and walked out the house to the neighbor's apartment.......

"YO RAMSES! HOLD UP!" That was my dawg Prichard screaming halfway across the school lawn. He came walking up, slow boppin' as he was known for. I swear he walked slower than a one legged human.

"Where you going for lunch man?"

"Man I got some snacks in my backpack bruh. I'm 'bout to sit under this tree and read for about half an hour." As always when I said that to anyone, I was looked at strange.

"Man bruh...you always reading. I swear you gonna turn into a bookmark or some shit one day. What's the lesson for today?" I reached in my backpack and pulled out a classic. Things Fall Apart.

"What's this shit about?," he asked, as he grabbed the book and started flippin' through the pages. I looked at him as strange as he looked at me.

"Bruh, you need to read up on ya history. Hell, look around on this campus. We are history." He just shook his head and laughed.

"Whatever my dude. Look, you enjoy this and I'm a go get something to eat. Yo, I'll holla at you in class." We dapped up, he took off and I made my way to a lowly tree near the entrance of the school. Being 16 wasn't easy I tell you. It's when everything started to almost turn into reality for a young adult. However, my world was very, very different. Here I was in a school with almost 2,500 kids, yet only a handful of us were black. I knew how the world was and how it treated us as a whole in society. In the back of my mind, even though I hadn't experienced any negativity since being here with these white folks, I knew it was here. My people are the minority. Here, I was beneath that term. I sat down and cracked open this masterpiece I was reading by Chinua Achebe.

"Okonkwo ruled his household with a heavy hand. His wives, especially the youngest, lived in perpetual
fear of his fiery temper and so did his little children.
Perhaps down in his heart Okonkwo was not a
cruel man, but his whole life was dominated by fear, the
fear of failure and of weakness."

As I read this portion of the book, I related the fear of the wives to the fear that I had within myself. My whole life was dominated by fear. Fear of rejection, fear of failure, fear of not being what I was supposed to be. That fear was being black.

The police came and wheeled my Uncle Ronnie out, sheet over his body, as he took a final ride over the concrete steps he had walked up for so many years. I recall riding down to the police station with the cops. Inside, I wasn't even scared. They talked to me, asking me questions about what I seen.

Nothing was accompanied with almost every response, because that's exactly what I seen. Nothing. After the dust settled and they saw that I had nowhere else to go, I was placed in custody of the state of Oklahoma. For the next two years, my life revolved solely around a group of strangers. I wasn't placed in a home. It was more of a giant shelter where we didn't have a care in the world. By the time I hit eight years old, I had gotten accustomed to my new found life. I had people I could play with everyday and books I could read so I was gravy. That's until the day that everything changed dramatically. As I was swingin' on the monkey bars one day on the playground, the director of the shelter called me inside.

"Congratulations Brian. We found a new home for you." I didn't comprehend what she was saying until I was led into a room where two random white people were standing, smiling from ear to ear.

"Hiiiiii Brian!" My eyes got big as I was wondering who this random woman was. She shouted my name as if I were a celebrity. To be honest, I thought she was high on some sort of drug. White folks were known to get wild off some X. She extended her hand out and I obliged, simply because I didn't know better.

"Do you like the name Ramses?" Scared to make her upset, I shook my head up and down.

"Great!," she clamored.

"Ramses Osiris Martin," the man behind her said. Before I was told anything, I figured that he was my new dad and this would be my new family. I was further made known of this when the director Ms. Willis sat me down and explained everything to me with them in the office. I wasn't sure why they changed my name. I wasn't sure as to where I would be living soon. All I knew is that a whole unchartered world was waiting for me. Days later, I found myself on a plane with them both. My new mom gave me a book on the flight.

"Now Ramses, read this. It's fun to learn."

"Okay," I said. It was a children's book about Ancient Egypt. It was nothing complicated as I understood everything in there. If only they knew how many books I read the last two years they would be astonished. What amazed me more than anything about this book were the pictures. The tombs, the caskets and the pyramids stood out to me. I never had seen anything like this in any book I ever read. It intrigued me. It opened my young mind. I didn't know it then, but this book would be the start of building me into a man. When it was all said and done.

I was now located in Newport Beach, CA. I indeed felt like I was transported into a different world. All I noticed were huge homes, with green lawns and a sunshine that rivaled any I had ever seen. It was a far cry from the rolling fields and brisk Midwest weather I had become accustomed to. The Boomer Sooner kid was now...I don't even know what you call people out here. I arrived at my new home which was a huge white mansion on a cliff, overlooking the Pacific Ocean. I didn't know what to think. I was only eight years old. What was I supposed to think? All I knew was that I still had a roof over my head, so I was grateful. Life had indeed taken a turn for me.

As I was winding down my day in school, the principal called me down to his office. I wasn't worried about anything, seeing that I didn't cause any problems here. I made my way down there, hoping to really hear news about more colleges that were offering me scholarships for football.

"Mr. Lyons," I said as I knocked on his door.

"Come on in Ramses. Have a seat." I sat down, patiently waiting as he finished up the last of his game of solitaire on the computer.

"Before we talk, I have a serious question for you."

"Well, I have a serious answer for you sir and I will be playing for Sparty in less than two years." He just chuckled.

"Naw. It's nothing to do with football. What is the reason behind your parents naming you Ramses?" I was so glad that he asked this, because I loved explaining it to people.

"Well, sir. Ramses is unique. Heck the whole aspect of my name is. My adoptive parents are big historians. Before they adopted me, they took a trip to Egypt, which is Ancient Kemet located in the Northeast corner of Alkebulan, which people call modern day Africa. They were awestruck by what they learned during that time. My birth name was Brian Carter. I was born to Byron and Brianna Carter. My new parents, they renamed me Ramses Osiris Martin when I was adopted. See Ramses was the founder of the 19th dynasty of Egypt. That's where my first name comes from. When my parents quote on quote found me, they believed I was the start of something extraordinary. Osiris, my middle name, was in honor of the Egyptian God Osiris. He was the God of the Dead, but also the God of agriculture. In agriculture, the planting and harvesting grain represents life and death in a crazy sort of way. So I was given that name to basically mean

"balance," as my parents wanted me to have a very balanced life. And Martin...well...that's just their last name." I folded my hands and kicked back. I loved telling that story.

"Interesting," he said, as he shook his head up and down.

"Now, onto business. Tell me what do you think about this?" He handed me a manila envelope. I took it, hoping it was a letter from East Lansing. I always loved Sparty since I started watching college football and I wanted to beat the shit out of Ohio State and Michigan one day. I just couldn't rock with any school who named themselves after a tree nut. Nor could I rock with a school that turned their backs on the athletes that made them millions. They had the Fab Five and made them out to be criminals. I looked at the envelope and it definitely wasn't college mail. I looked up at Mr. Lyons with a weird look.

"Well go ahead," as he shooed his hand at me, anxious for me to open it. I ripped it open and started to read the contents inside.

"Project R.E.B.O.R.N. sir? What the hell is this? I don't get it."

"Well, Ramses, this here I think would be a great opportunity for a student like you to touch those who don't get to live in our world on a regular basis. We're privileged, we really are. You know everyone who lives here makes good money, has running water and doesn't have to worry about where their next meal is coming from. Not everyone is so fortunate. I think two weeks with this program will enhance your mind farther than what it already is. You are a heck of a student-athlete, but life lessons will take you farther than any grade or football could ever do. A textbook is nothing but written words on a page. As a matter of fact, excuse my French, but it's a bunch of souped up bullshit they sell to the youth. The education you need to succeed won't be found there." I looked down at the letter again, fiddling with it really.

"So what does this consist of sir?"

"Well, it consists of you moving in with a family for two weeks, in or out of state, depending on where the program feels you will fit in. From there, you will work within their community to help them enhance in any way possible. So...do you think you will be interested?" It was kind of cool, but scary at the same time I thought. I necessarily didn't have the knack to impose on people I didn't even know. But then again, I kind of did the same thing in my life, except I was brought in.

"I'll let you know tomorrow sir."

"Okay Ramses. Thanks a lot and I'll see you tomorrow." I walked out of Mr. Lyons office and headed towards my last class of the day, thinking about how this would factor into the enhancement of my life. This trip was scheduled to occur over spring break. At 16, we don't necessarily think of spending spring break being an aid to someone we don't know. That's the two weeks we want to just chill with friends. I had a decision to make. Reading a book on Buddhism before, I remember one particular quote that Buddha said that always stuck with me. It was "Know well what leads you forward and what holds you back, and choose the path that leads to wisdom."

Gaining wisdom was all too much of a distant memory in this world we were embroiled in today. People were always searching for the next hidden treasure or the next great monument that wasn't discovered. The next greatest athletic superstar or the next great technological invention that would change the world. No one wanted to search for wisdom, which was a gift that every individual should break their necks trying to search for. It even says in Proverbs 4: 6-7, Do not forsake wisdom, and she will protect you; love her, and she will watch over you. Wisdom is supreme; therefore get wisdom. Though it cost all you have, get understanding.

My decision was made before I walked back into that classroom. Not the decision to relax with a random family. Just the decision to not fear what I may not have understood. I went home that early afternoon, ate dinner and relaxed. It was a chill Thursday. My parents would be back Saturday, as they were in Greece doing archaeological work. That was their life's passion. Mr. and Mrs. Daniel Martin. Two history buffs who met while they were in college, always seeking out to explore the mysteries of those who had come before us.

It was strange at times to have parents like that. I didn't even consider my biological mom and dad whom I had lost years ago when I was only four years old. That's how far my mind had left them in the past. They weren't what you would exactly call model class citizens, as both were involved in the drug game. I used to think as a three or four year old that our "family trips" were amazing. We would always end up in another city every single weekend it seemed. Motel after motel, my parents always made it seem like Disneyland was right around the corner from where we were staying. I never understood it back then. As I grew older and wiser, I realize that I was just extra added baggage on their joy ride.

Then, the one joy ride they didn't take me on to Houston, that's where they met their demise. Their car was found upside down on the side of the I-10, burnt to a crisp. My uncle always told me that daddy just lost control of the wheel. I think he however lost control of his life and someone took it. Regardless of what was true or not, they were gone and I was here. Life continued on. Five o'clock rolled around. After I had my fill of the news, I cut the TV off, walked upstairs and headed to my parents book collection. I pulled out one about the Greek philosopher Socrates, who was known as the Godfather of Western Philosophy. The thing that stood out about him to me was how he challenged all of his students to come to their own understanding of different issues. It was like he challenged them to challenge their own beliefs. He never wrote a book himself, but it amazed me how he indeed impacted the world, which was proven by the numerous number of books that people wrote on his life.

I sat there for the next two hours, dissecting page upon page, soaking my brain up with knowledge. As 7:30 hit, I walked outside. The sun had already descended beneath the horizon as I stood above the earth, looking down at the moonlit Pacific Ocean. I began to think about the unexplored chapters in my life. All I knew was this. Oklahoma was out of my mind permanently. Newport Beach was home. That was just in my literal sense though. In a physical sense, I had yet to find home. The true spirit that resided in me walked my blood stained arteries and traveled my veins at max speed, looking for home. I was a black kid in a world that most of mines weren't accustomed to. Who was I? I knew it wasn't a rich kid. I had not yet discovered the other side. When I say the other side, I am not talking about being poor. I have yet to meet the other side of life.

I was still on the child's end. I patiently waited for the day that I could see the grown man side, which would allow my thinking and wisdom to grow even more. We are human and built up by experience and circumstance. Some had come, but I would be stupid to think that the biggest challenge in my life came when I moved out here. I yearned for that. Hopefully, when I would see Mr. Lyons tomorrow, I would hope that a journey to find the inner being would commence. My name was Ramses, but I had yet to sit on my throne and conquer the land as the Great Kings that I bared the name of had done once upon a time.

"Where will I be going Mr. Lyons???"

"That Ramses...I have no idea. That's up to the good people who run the program." I continued engaging him as we sat in his office this early Thursday morning discussing what would come of this.

"I do know one thing though," he stated. "You will know where you will be going by the end of today. Are you parents back?"

"They return Saturday sir."

"Okay. I know them well. With the way they travel and explore, they will definitely agree with this. It's gets you away from home for a while and allows you to find comfort in helping others."

"Cool beans," I told him, getting up to exit the office and

head to class.

"**WAIT! THERE'S ONE LAST THING!**" I turned around ever so quickly.

"What's that sir?"

"The staff at Michigan State requested your tapes." A huge grin came across his face as did mines. I finished out my morning classes and got ready to do my usual for lunch. Heading over to my favorite tree, I continued on reading

"Things Fall Apart." I was at peace with myself when I had a book in my hands. I had gotten so indulged in the book that I completely was oblivious to the school bells signaling the end of the lunch period. I stuffed my book back in my bag. As I got up, all I heard was *"RAM BABY RAM!"* from a car full of girls at my school that were driving by. Being a star football player had its perks I tell you. As I headed back towards the school, I saw a bunch of strange people surrounding someone outside. I started to freak out a lil bit, hoping that it wasn't one of my friends that were hurt. I ran up to the scene to find Prichard down on the ground in pain. I tried to make my way through the crowd, but the amount of bodies around him held me at bay.

"Calm down, Calm down. You're okay." That's all I heard as I slowly began to find myself at ease with the arrival of EMT's. Through my obscured vision, I could see Mr. Lyons talking to what looked like the police.

"Looks like a laceration that is right above the eye. Let's get him to the ambulance for treatment." I was worried sick about my peoples. Especially since I didn't know what caused his injury. After about 20 minutes, I crept on over to the ambulance, completely oblivious to the fact that I had missed half of my fifth hour already.

"There you go. All stitched up."

"I had a headache from hell bruh," he told me, as the EMT's turned to see me.

"What happened man?," I asked him.

"Man...I don't even know to tell you the truth. I was down tying my shoe. I heard **"NIGGER BOY"** and everything went black." I looked over at the EMT to make sure this fool wasn't delusional and just spitting out a story for dramatics.

"What's going on sir?," I asked one of the medics.

"Well your friend here got hit with a good kick in the face or some heavy object, causing him to have a nice gash above his eyebrow. Probably some ignorant kids, because we don't condone this type of behavior in this city." I wasn't understanding what he meant until I seen the tree. There, with the uniformed officers, was a noose hanging from a branch. I never thought racism was dead, but I had yet to become a victim of it. Nothing protects you from being black. Not even being the high school football star, all state selection and National Honor Society member. None of that matters.

To a lot of people, all they see are villains. Television, radio and other sources have contributed to that image, but that's not what represents us. College graduates, successful businessmen, authors, poets and motivators. Those are the characteristics that define us. I know there were cameras all around the school. I didn't care though. Whether it was a scared punk inside the school, or some grown ass adult, I didn't want to know who it was. I wasn't scared when I came here and I wouldn't be instilled with fear now. Trust, I wasn't worried.

Back in school, I waltzed back into Mr. Lyons office. He had already notified my parents, who had already landed in Florida and would be here tomorrow morning instead of Saturday. When I talked to my mom in the office, she was hysterical and upset. I could hear my dad yelling in the background. Regardless of my skin tone I was their son, and they were going to go to war for me, even if it meant giving up everything they had. If one crazy person attacked one black kid, then they figured that I could be next in line. I know everyone looked at white people as always having a hidden agenda. Not every one of them is like that; just like every brother you come across isn't a menace to society.

"First off Ram, I am so sorry for the ignorance of today. You are a great kid and I promise you whoever the person or persons who did this to Prichard will be held accountable. We have every tape being reviewed right now."

"Man Mr. Lyons," as I scratched my head. "I'm not worried about that. If I worry about the outside world, then how can I have inner peace?" He just folded his hands and shook his head.

"Ramses, I am going to be straight up with you." He got up to shut his office door, as I knew then that I was about to hear something serious.

"I never judged anyone one day in my life. I made it to Newport Beach by way of Brick City years ago." I looked at him strange as hell.

"Yea, I know that look. People are shocked when I tell them that."

"Newark sir?"

"Yup. I grew up in Newark. The only white kid in an all black neighborhood. They gave me all kinds of nicknames like coke, lil white and all sorts of other mumbo jumbo. My parents were poor and they did what they could. I somehow made it to Rutgers and earned a degree in Education. Years later, here I am living my dream in a city that I could only dream of as a child. To be honest, I never heard of Newport Beach until I got the job offer. Then I see you. One of a handful of black youth here. And I know what's going through your mind. I went through the same thing, except of course, my skin tone is about 100 shades lighter. So you know how they say never assume?" I was awestruck at this revelation. I really didn't know dude had came from where he came from. It was enlightening to say the least.

"Mr. Lyons. Any word on where I'll be going for the next two weeks?" He just smiled.

"Already focused on the next big thing I see. Here." He handed me an envelope. I immediately opened it up and read its contents.

Dear Ramses,

Thank you for volunteering your spring break to help a community in need. Enclosed is an airline ticket. You will be heading to Birmingham, Alabama for community relations projects. Thank you again and enjoy your trip.

Sarah,

V.P. Project R.E.B.O.R.N.

"Birmingham Sir?"

"Yep, good ol' country Alabama. It says you leave Tuesday and you've had a long enough day. Head home and relax. Your parents will be here tomorrow. Don't even come in. I'll have them mark you as a medical case. You just prep for your big trip. Remember, change only comes when it is started from the inside." I alternated my vision between him and the letter.

"Maybe I need Birmingham more than Birmingham needs me sir. I'm out." I walked out the door, focused on what was next to come. That night, as I lie in a silent house, doing my usual reading with the television on in the background, the image on the screen distracted me. I knew this movie and scene without sound like I knew the back of my hand. Tre and Ricky had started to walk towards opposite sides of the alley. All of a sudden, a car full of Bloods pulled up. Tre turned around.

"**RICKY!**," he screamed. Ricky ran for his life, but to no avail. Those shots pierced through his back and took his life right there. I un-muted the TV and put that book down, finishing out Boyz in the Hood.

"**TURN YO PUNK ASS OVER!**" Doughboy hovering over Ferris always did something to me. Every time I saw that, I always pondered one question. Did my parent's killers do them the same way? To this day, I still don't believe they died in a car accident. It didn't bother me to the point to where I was in a depression every night about it. I did want answers though. Unfortunately, I knew I would never get them. After the movie went off, I went outside, looking at the water from my cliff side residence.

I started to wonder about Birmingham. It wasn't so much about the violence or country way of living that I would have to get acclimated too. I was more so thinking would I be black enough for my own people. I know that may have sounded rhetorical, but it was indeed a very logical question. I sat down in the reclining chair and leaned back into my own world. I closed my eyes and just started to imagine myself in a different world.

"**RAMSES!!!**" I shot up in a panic, flailing my arms and kicking as if I were trying to escape the death grip of a shark.

"**RAMSES CALM DOWN!!!**" It was my mom, trying to grab me and contain me. I finally got calm and caught my breath. I also noticed the bright sun shining dead in my eyes.

"Mom...whew...mom. I'm sorry."

"Are you okay hun? Oh my goodness. I was so worried about you." She barraged me with kiss after kiss after kiss.

"Oh Dandelion give it a rest. Let him breathe." My dad didn't talk much when my mom smothered me, but those words were much needed at this time.

"Mom, I'm alright."

"No, No. Come in the house so we can talk." I happily obliged. Not so much because of my parents, but because this sun had kicked my tail and was closing in on a fatality. We talked for a good two hours over a hearty morning breakfast consisting of my mom's special biscuits and gravy recipe. I swear it tasted like heaven on a plate. Everything was put out on the table from the incident to Michigan State football, to me leaving for Birmingham Tuesday morning. They weren't nervous. I was grateful too, because the one battle they could never understand, I was about to face it head on and I needed some strength in my corner to motivate me to do what I had to do. It wasn't chess right now. It was checkers. Simple and plain. I just had to make sure that I didn't make it too complicated.

By the time Sunday rolled around, I was damn near ready. I went over to the mall that day just to make one final roundabout as to what I might need. I know it was hot as hell here, but spring in the South is different. Hell, I wouldn't be surprised if it was still chilly down there during this time of year. Cold or chill was something I never was accustomed to, seeing that it rarely dipped below 70 degrees out here. I soaked in everything from the sunshine, to the numerous amounts of people carrying their dogs and having their babies on a leash. Yes, I said that right. It sounded ass backwards, but they were strange like that out here in Newport Beach. I guess all the millions upon millions people made out here did something dramatic to their minds, like forget who the human was.

That probably was the only thing that I never really got used to while living out here. At times, I became oblivious to the world outside of me which couldn't even muster up $5 for something to eat. It may sound wrong and heartless, but ask yourself this. Do you not conform to a way that you have known most of your life? For 99.9% of us, it happens. It's not saying we don't empathize with the next man's plight, but everyone's operation is different based on the environment they are encompassed in. People in the higher class only want to see higher class things. People in impoverished countries only know the ways of survival through the hardships they face. It's not to say they don't wanna strive to make it, but your environment builds a certain character inside of you as an individual. I had only hoped that within two weeks, I would understand a totally different world and have a whole new appreciation for the life I had been given.

I arrived into Birmingham without a glitch. The flight was smooth and southern hospitality was an understatement. I thought by getting off the plane in some slacks, a vest and a tie would have people staring at me awkwardly. It was the exact opposite. The compliments of *"you look nice" and "Good creases"* took me by surprise. It was the second culture shock that I had ever experienced. Newport people and Southern California folks in general didn't waste their time giving you compliments. They were clad out in so many different types of fashion that they really didn't care how you were dressed. All they cared about was the nightlife and up tempo lifestyle.

It was fourteen of us and I was one of only two black kids on the trip. I wasn't anti social, seeing that I engaged with the whole group on the way here. I still felt out of place. We were now at baggage claim with our bags in hand, ready to bounce. Our guide Mr. Lile was talking to who I assumed was the head of the R.E.B.O.R.N. project down here.

"Ramses!?," he called me over. Honestly, it felt kind of awkward that he would call the black kid over to meet another black individual.

"This is Mrs. Debra Dockery, head of R.E.B.O.R.N. in Birmingham."

"Hello ma'am. Ramses." She stuck her hand out and shook

my hand with little to no effort.

"Charmed," she replied. The look she gave me was one of disgust and no trust. I didn't know what I had did to her, but whatever I did, she certainly let me know that she wasn't fond of me at all.

"I will talk to the entire group one on one on Wednesday morning Eric. For now, we have the bus waiting outside to take them to their hotel. Why don't you let Mr. Ramses lead the way. I think he will be able to lead you wherever with no qualms." I knew subliminal shots and it wasn't any secret as to what was going on. Have the big, black, burly guy lead the pack so everyone else could be intimidated. I was born at night and not last night. I ain't gone lie, it irked my soul that I was going through this. All I wanted to do was come to help. I didn't want to be seen as the token black kid with the silver spoon.

We boarded the bus and headed off to the hotel. I threw on my Beats and just zoned out to some old N.W.A. I was in my own world, hoping and praying that these two weeks would go by without a hiccup. I researched Birmingham before I got here. Down south hospitality was one thing, but this place had a dark side. It was violent down here. Every gang you could imagine claimed turf out here. Thefts, robberies, murder, it all happened in the Magic City. Everyone has this misconception when it comes to states like Alabama or Mississippi. People have this notion that nothing but good ol boys resides down in these parts. Forrest Gump may have fooled millions, but I wasn't stupid enough to fall in the assumption trap.

We finally arrived at the Sheraton, which wasn't too far from the campus of the University of Alabama–Birmingham. The first thing I noticed was how this was indeed a farfetched journey from the high rolling hills. I wasn't in Kansas anymore and Dorothy looked like this was where she met her demise at. We walked off the bus as our luggage was being handed out to us from under the bus.

"I'm assuming this is yours with the big Cincinnati Reds on it huh partna?" I kind of looked at dude strange for a minute.

"Yea, that's mine." He snickered as he handed it to me.

"Newport beach though? Ain't no bangin' there, but nice try. Enjoy ya trip." I didn't know what to say. I was literally awestruck. All I had was a bag from the logo of my favorite team and it was mistaken for something else. It was an uneasy feeling. I wasn't here to make enemies. I was here to help. I was here to uplift. I was here to try and learn something about a group of people in a state that I had never visited before.

As I picked up my bag and turned around, I then realized that by the end of this trip, the biggest lesson that I would learn would be about me. The good thing about this trip was that we all had our own rooms, so I could unwind, just have time for me and pray in secrecy when I needed to. This wasn't like normal school trips where you thought kids would be getting down and dirty. We were selected because we were quote on quote the best of the best. In laymen terms, we were rich kids who didn't cause trouble anywhere we went. No one was expecting any foul activity or rude behavior from us.

Before we departed to our rooms for the evening, we were told that all activities would start Wednesday morning. Being informed on how busy we were going to be, it was advised that we eat up and get all the rest we could, because 10 a.m. would be here faster than we knew. We would eat dinner complimentary of the hotel tonight and just be able to relax. I got to room #219 and just threw everything down on the floor. I jumped on the bed and just closed my eyes, trying to imagine what this experience would be like after two weeks were up. It was only a tad bit past three in the afternoon, so I had time to unwind. I didn't want to call my parents yet. I wanted to really soak in the whole experience. When I say that, I am talking about the black experience.

It was evident from what had transpired that I wasn't considered the typical black teenager. I was here with a bunch of privileged white kids from a place where the only negative thing that occurred was when a dog was cradled as a baby and an actual baby was put on a leash. I didn't ask for my circumstances. All I could do was embrace them. I wasn't sitting around in a temporary home wishing that someone would come and rescue me. No, not at all. I simply adapted and dealt with the cards that I was dealt. To be as young as I was and have that thought process, it put me ahead of many other people. We try and try to change things, or wish for better. It's okay to wish for better, but we have to look at the bigger picture. God sometimes has to take us through some things so that we may appreciate where we will end up.

I remember when I first started elementary school in Newport. I was literally the only black kid in the whole darn school. There were stares not due to negativity, but simply because I was different. Truthfully, I couldn't blame them. It was the same way that if you went into a business meeting for a Fortune 500 company and everyone was wearing suits, you would look oddly at the person who came in wearing sandals, Speedos, shades and a tank top. If there was any negative ill will towards me, I certainly didn't see it. I was eight years old. All I saw was the playground and lunchtime. The white kids in my school would always ask me what it was like where I came from. I didn't get into the whole story of my parents, as they didn't need to know that. I simply painted Hugo, Oklahoma as the most beautiful place on the face of the earth. They were city kids that became awestruck by the country. How we used to have old milk crates serve as basketball rims hanging off of a light pole. How we chased lightning bugs, captured them, took the light off of their body and pretended it was a ring to put on. Tornadoes were tornadoes, but they swore it was the greatest thing since sliced bread. I was truly happy to be a country boy at heart, even with spending my pre teenage and teenage years in the city. Now, I was feeling the pressures of another struggle. It was the am I black enough struggle. I shouldn't have to question this, but the looks from earlier let me know that the world wouldn't always be your friend, even if you have the same melanin pigmentation in your skin.

Grown people looking down at a kid isn't cool, but it's worst when the assumption is made that your life has been the easiest. In the inner city, my people struggle with poverty, drugs, gangs and the constant threat of getting killed by the police because you were walking while black. For me, my struggle came in the fact that I was separated from my culture.

Even being as close as I was to Los Angeles, I had never strayed towards Watts, South Central, Compton or any other place that the world assumed was negative. I wanted badly to just visit and make friends from those areas, but I felt deep down that I wouldn't be accepted because of who I was. I was a black kid that was raised in suburban white America. One time at the age of 13, I was on a field trip with my junior high school. My school and a bunch of other schools from L.A. and Orange County took their football players to The Coliseum for a meet and greet with the USC football team. We met current greats and past greats. I really wanted to meet Reggie Bush, but seeing how that school shammed him, I unfortunately couldn't. That even made it scarier for me to want to go to a university for sports and take in the whole college experience. If they could do him dirty like that, after leading them to two national titles, making them millions and literally being the human highlight reel for three years, then what would a school do to me when I had my opportunity to shine in the national spotlight? We were running cone drills on the field. I had on my Cincinnati Reds T shirt, some black shorts and some red cleats.

Red was my favorite color and I was impervious to any gang culture because I didn't experience it. I knew about it, but seeing how it never directly affected me, I literally was innocent. As I jogged off the field behind the bleachers during a break to get some water, I saw three brothers over there huddled around the water fountain.

"What's going on fellas?," I said as I walked up to wait my turn. All three looked at me with a menacing stare, but the third one who was drinking water intimidated me the most. His mouth was in the water and his eyes were on me. He finished up and walked right up to me.

"What's brackin Blood? Leuders Park Bompton Piru nigga." I ain't know what any of that meant, but I knew it wasn't cool.

"How you tryna flash the set nigga? You ain't from round nowhere hood my nigga." The other two started laughin' and I was terribly confused.

"Man bruh, I just like the Cincinnati Reds. I'm from Newport. I'm just trying to introduce myself. Ramses." All three of 'em started laughing in my face. I mean, it was one of those Bernie Mac just ripped up the stage type of laughs.

"Nigga what you some type of Egyptian prince or some shit?" They laughed even harder.

"The fuck Blood. Yo, you gone part the Red Sea nigga?" The laugher got even louder. Inside of my head, I was saddened by their ignorance that they didn't even know that Ramses wasn't the one who parted the Red Sea. Then, things got serious once again. "Beat this thru yo' brain Blood. You ain't one of the homies. I swear if these faculty wasn't here right now we'd bop off on ya ass nigga. We don't like yo kind nigga. Oh, Oh, you thought cause you saw three niggas together that you was automatically one of us? Fuck yo life blood. Matter fact, Imma stop callin' you blood cause you ain't one, will never be one. More importantly, you ain't a hood nigga so roll the fuck outta my face." I saw all three of them ball up their fists and I calmly walked away from the water fountain. I finished up the drills that day, but I was definitely shaken by everything that had transpired.

As I got back on the bus headed back to school that day, I sat all the way in the back by my lonesome. I looked at my skin. I started to question whether or not God made the mistake of making me black. I couldn't appease my own people. When I got home that night, I played it off good to my parents. I told them how I had met Ken Norton Sr., Troy Polamalu, Marcus Allen and a bunch of other football greats. When I got to my room though, I simply cried. I cried in my pillow. I was starting to wish that I wasn't black. I kind of wished that when I got adopted by white parents that my skin tone would change like theirs. I wasn't accepted by my own and I felt rejected. In actuality, that incident made me stray farther and farther from my culture. I slowly but surely took my focus away from hip hop music and anything associated with black culture.

Then, that's when I saw it. In the corner of my room, my parents had left a book in there about Ancient Egypt. I read it and became fascinated. I must've only left my room that night to piss and eat. I read for God knows how long. I figured if my own were gonna say I was history in their eyes, I might as well put some history in front of my eyes. That's how I became a history buff. When my own wanted me history, I started to embrace my history. If it was one good thing that came from that incident, it was the fact that I learned that knowledge of self was great. I carried that mindset all the way into high school. From freshmen year, I was the lone wolf on the team. I came in my ninth grade year at 6'1 and a solid 220.

Immediately, I channeled anger into something positive and took football as my personal outlet. I endured the *"You ain't one of us"* talk whenever we played an inner city school. I was gravy though, because my mind had matured to the point of where I couldn't be fazed by any one of my own crucifying me for how my life turned out to be. Now, I was back at square one at this hotel.

"How is everything Ram?" That was my father on the phone as I was telling him how excited I was about this trip. I hid from him the two negative aspects and just focused on the positive that I knew would come. We chopped it up for a good thirty minutes, with two of those minutes being my mom saying she missed me like two billion times.

As I hung up the phone, I saw it was nearing four o'clock. We were meeting in the hotel restaurant at five for dinner, so I had major time to blow. ***"Knock, knock."*** I got up to answer the door.

"Sup boy." It was my man's Carlos, the only other brother with me on this trip. He was an implant from Oakland. His parents had expanded their business to the point of where they didn't have to struggle on the rough and rugged streets of that city anymore.

"So man what's up. What you think about this country life?," he asked. I just chuckled.

"You know I'm from the country man. This ain't nothing new. Lemme ask you something though."

"Sup?," he replied.

"Do you ever feel some type of way about having to leave Oakland to live in the hills of Newport Beach?" He didn't respond immediately. He simply put his hand on his chin as if he were thinking of the right response.

"Well...Ram. This is how I see it. I grew up in East Oakland. Right there on Seminary. Where we from, we call it the cemetery. Dead bodies get strung up all day and all night over there. I know pops was trying to crack into the internet marketing game, but really, let's face it. The world looks at that stuff as a pyramid scheme, so not too many people from the hood were rocking with it. I mean to keep it 100, who from the hood got $500 just to invest and try to start their own business. Not the folks I grew up around I'll tell you that much. When pops took that risk, he struggled mightily. He would drive to Frisco and the burbs in his best clothes to try and sell this idea of a better future. Moms wasn't too happy or excited about it, but they been together since high school and she was gonna stick by her man no matter what. This all happened when I was 11.

Over the next four years, he gradually built a team and now pops is a six, damn near seven figure earner. I think about all the people who laughed and mocked him, talking about a pyramid scheme. But when you look at a regular 9 to 5, that's a pyramid scheme in itself. You got the workers at the bottom. Follow that by the managers, supervisors, heads of the department, the heads over all the departments, vice president, president and then CEO. That is a pyramid in itself.

When we finally moved down here the day after my 14th birthday, I was sad. I didn't know anyone. What I was used to was gone for good. Hell, I was really upset at the fact that I was no longer a hood nigga. And that's sad. Think about it. I got sad because I wouldn't be considered a hood nigga anymore. Then, after about four months out here, I thought to myself. Why am I saddened by the fact that I ain't in poverty anymore? Its like we get so accustomed to one environment that we think that is supposed to be how we live our whole lives. We try so hard to be hood niggas when we fail to realize is that our parents are working their asses off so that we will never ever have to come back to the hood. I had to let that sink in and marinate. I haven't been back to Oakland since. Pops flew some family down to Newport a while back. They were amazed. Yet at the same time, I read their vibe. As mom and pops was taking them out to dinner, I could feel the hate they had inside of them. The oh you think you're all that cause you can pay for all of our meals type attitudes. I knew it was there, but I couldn't fathom it anymore.

"What I'm saying to you man is this. When I met you, I thought you were a square ass nigga who was privileged and didn't know anything about being a brother. When I grew up mentally, I saw you only as my brother. Our struggles were two different ones, but we both struggled. Don't let them tell you, NO ONE, that you ain't black. Cause I guarantee the police gone be watching our ass no matter where we are at in life. Especially me. I still got Oakland in me. Got the dreads and a gold grill that I rock in school. Hey, I'm like Marshawn Lynch some days. I just go there so I don't get fined. They gone say what they gone say. Just be you."

He balled up his fist and signaled for a fist pound. I definitely pounded my boy up as we spent the next thirty minutes just rapping back and forth to each other. As five hit, we strolled downstairs and met the rest of the group in the restaurant. The worst thing you could ever do is give a bunch of teenagers a big ol' buffet to choose from. Crab legs, steak, shrimp, mussels, prime rib, biscuits, calamari, salmon, clams, egg drop soup, orange chicken and it was just crazy how all this food was just here for my disposal. Man, I was literally in heaven. We sat there and got our money's worth, even though we didn't spend a dime. Me and Carlos had four plates by ourselves, with one of mines being nothing but shrimp. That salt and pepper squid was serving me well also. After a good two hours down there chilling and stuffing my face, I made my way back to my room to indulge in a book. It wasn't just any book, but indeed one that would transfix the mind. I say that because it was read in prison by the great Malcolm X himself. Mr. By Any Means Necessary. Now that was a brother who faced the opposition head on. He motivated me to do great things in life. As I cracked open The Souls of Black Folks by W.E.B. Dubois, my mind shifted from religion to reality. I began to read a passage from the book that stuck out to me vividly.

That such an institution was unthinkable in 1870 was due in part to certain acts of the Freedmen's Bureau itself. It came to regard its work as merely temporary and Negro suffrage as a final answer to all present perplexities. The political ambition of many of its agents and protégés led it far afield into questionable activities, until the South, nursing its own deep prejudices, came easily to ignore all the good deeds of the Bureau and hate its very name with perfect hatred. So the Freedmen's Bureau died, and its child was the Fifteenth Amendment.

The passing of a great human institution before its work is done, like the untimely passing of a single soul, but leaves a legacy of striving for other men. The legacy of the Freedmen's Bureau is the heavy heritage of this generation. Today, when new and vaster problems are destined to strain every fiber of the national mind and soul, would it not be well to count this legacy honestly and carefully? For this much all men know: despite compromise, war, and struggle, the Negro is not free. In the backwoods of the Gulf States, for miles and miles, he may not leave the plantation of his birth; in well-nigh the whole rural South the black farmers are peons, bound by law and custom to an economic slavery, from which the only escape is death or the penitentiary. In the most cultured sections and cities of the South the Negroes are a segregated servile caste, with restricted rights and privileges. Before the courts, both in law and custom, they stand on a different and peculiar basis.

Taxation without representation is the rule of their political life. And the result of all this is, and in nature must have been, lawlessness and crime. That is the large legacy of the Freedmen's Bureau, the work it did not do because it could not. I have seen a land right merry with the sun, where children sing, and rolling hills lie like passioned women wanton with harvest. And there in the King's Highways sat and sits a figure veiled and bowed, by which the traveler's footsteps hasten as they go. On the tainted air broods fear. Three centuries' thought has been the raising and unveiling of that bowed human heart, and now behold a century new for the duty and the deed. The problem of the Twentieth Century is the problem of the color-line.

I loved books like this that told you about history, but at the same time taught you how to think beyond the spectrum. If only so many more of us would open our minds up to what is not in our comfort zone, we would reach a zone that many never step into because of fear. I was blessed to have this thinking ability for a 16 year old kid. In another year, I would graduate and hopefully be headed to Michigan State to play for Sparty and crew. However, in this time, I needed to continue to build up my mental, because my life would not be defined by what occurs on the football field. It will be defined by what I accomplished as a man in the field of inspiring acts that I invoked upon the masses. I read the book all the way until eight o'clock and stopped to go into deep thought and prayer. I had a vision of building an empire. I would be the one that would transcend man and draw people to me. I wanted to be the one people raved about, but never seen. I learned that the best thing anyone can do is play in the background. I didn't have to be in the front taking all the limelight. I was ok with not being seen, because the most inspiring things that occur in this world happen when no one is watching. I cut on the TV and just flipped through the channels.

I was excited about tomorrow. It would break me out of a mold and form me into something new. Whether negative or positive, I knew that my life would change starting at 10 a.m. on a Wednesday morning. I cut off all the lights and lie in my bed with a smile on my face. You could say I wasn't your definition of black, but don't tell me that I ain't black. Black transcends. Black is what started this earth. Light came out of darkness, which is black. Light can't escape a black hole. Black is indeed powerful in every facet that you could imagine. Black is the color of the soil where forest grows. You want it pitch black when you sleep so that you can sleep in peace. Therefore, black is peaceful. Black is tranquility. Black is unique. When you mix all the colors of paint together, you get black. Black is the lasting color. Simply put, black is beautiful and I would definitely see if beauty was only in the eye of the beholder starting tomorrow. I closed my eyes and anxiously awaited the challenge that tomorrow would bring.

I arose at eight o'clock on the dot Wednesday morning. I wasn't a morning person at all, so thank goodness no one was around me to feel the wrath of my grouchy ways. There I lay, pondering in my head on how day one of this two week excursion was going to be. Time went by slow as I didn't move a muscle until 8:30 a.m. There were two knocks at my door, followed by an envelope that was slid beneath it. It was from Debra Dockery, the head of the R.E.B.O.R.N. project out here in Birmingham. I opened it up and read its contents. Through all the fluff, I saw one sentence that stood out vividly. "Stay together and do not go anywhere without a community leader." Once I seen the location, I knew exactly why. We were headed to Ensley. It was time to see what the other side of the world looked like first hand.

On TV, you could only imagine so much. They painted the people of that section out to be monsters. If you don't know what I am talking about, just watch the First 48 on A&E. They are always on there. Me, I learned a long time ago not to judge a book by its cover. The hood had murders, but the suburbs had murders as well. You just don't know how many predominantly white suburbs have a drug problem in their community. The difference is that they just keep theirs under wraps and don't have it exposed to the media as often. Why? The flow of money, that's why. In the black community, it's almost an everyday headline. The media feeds what they know will cause hate and discontent.

Just look at the black neighborhoods of today. On every corner you will find two things. Churches and liquor stores. The quote on quote Christian slave owners from way back when used the Bible to validate the evil that they were doing. They used that power of religion. Somehow, it all stayed with my people. Once the crack era of the 80's popped off, what better way to fuel drugs than with liquor? It's a sad statistic, but it's damn near true everywhere you go in the inner city.

I showered up real quick and threw on my clothes. Once 9:30 hit, I made my way down to the lobby to see that half of the people on the trip were already down there.

"Are you ready for this?," Mr. Lile asked me.

"Ready as I'm ever gonna be sir." A smile came across his face and he placed his hand on my shoulder.

"To tell you the truth Ramses," he whispered. "I honestly in my God given spirit think you are the only one who is made for this trip."

"What do you mean sir?" He walked me to the corner of the lobby and continued to speak.

"Look, for the most part, besides Carlos, these kids don't know anything about being poor or living in dire circumstances. All they know is what they see on television. Now, I am not saying they aren't genuine in their actions. However, I can guarantee some of them will go home with the *"it ain't me"* mentality. And that's what I truly feel needs to stop in this world. Saying it's not me doesn't mean that it doesn't affect you. If my fellow man is down, then it is my human duty to try and bring him back up. I can't save every individual, but I can do my part. Look at this." He reached in his wallet, pulled out a picture and handed it to me.

"THESE YOUR PARENTS?!" He nodded his head up and down.

"Adopted, with two black brothers and a Puerto Rican sister, in the heart of North Philly. You're made for this." They say that a picture can say a thousand words, but that one spoke about one billion words to me. He walked away and I was left thinking to myself that everything would work out according to God's plan. I went over and got me a ham croissant made as I waited for the rest of the group to show up.

10 o'clock came with the quickness. With no instructions given to us except follow Mr. Lile to the bus, we were on our way into unfamiliar territory. It had the feeling of myself being eight years old again. For me, leaving Oklahoma with two strangers for a rich new land was the scariest journey of my young life. I remember when I landed at LAX with my new family. It was a culture shock unlike any other I had ever experienced. I saw so many different breeds of people and it was beyond intimidating. I wasn't so much in fear of the

unknown. I was more in fear of if I was going to make it. Here I was, déjà vu all over again.

The bus took off from the hotel as I drifted into my own world with my Beats on. I had "I Keep Forgetting" by Michael Mcdonald playing. For y'all that don't know, this was the song with the same beat that Warren G used on his smash hit "Regulate" way back when in the 90's. It was a perfect zone out song that gave me goose bumps and just prepared me for anything. They say music is the cure to the soul. For me, it was a cure that I couldn't explain. If I had cancer, music should cure me from it. We kept rollin' and rollin' until we finally came to a stop. I raised my head up and looked out of the window. This for damn sure didn't look like no hood and it for damn sure didn't look like anyone was suffering over here. Mr. Lile and Ms. Dockery exited the bus, walking over to a group of white folks. Outside of a large building. Carlos slid on over to my seat.

"Man if these fools struggling than an anteater ain't eatin ants anymore." I was with him. What kind of foolery was this I thought. We just sat and stared while the others kept talking away, looking like they were in heaven still.

"Ok you all," Mr. Lile said. "You can all exit the bus now." I didn't wanna get off of this. I came here for a transformation and all it looked like I got was a transport to the Newport Beach of Alabama.

"Kids," Ms. Dockery said. "Inside waiting are the families that will take you in for two weeks. You have no worries. The Southside of Birmingham has nothing but affluent homes with the best of facilities for all of your needs." Before she could utter another word, I raised my hand.

"Yes Mr. Martin." With the way she said that, she did nothing but piss me off even more.

"I'm sorry ma'am and excuse my French, but what in the good fuck are we doing over here?"

"RAMSES!," Mr. Lile said. I wasn't tryna hear it though.

"Naw, naw. This is bullshit. You fly us all the way out here from Richville, U.S.A. where we got it made. You tell us we are here to help someone who doesn't have it as good as us. And we end up in a clone of our own city. That's the problem with this damn country. You create fluff to make things sound good. In reality, you don't even give a damn. And you," as I pointed to Ms. Dockery. "You a sister and you acting like we don't exist!"

"RAMSES COME HERE," as Mr. Lile clinched his hand around my arm and drug me off to the side. "That is a grown woman there and you need to show some respect."

"No Mr. Lile," I whispered back. "This is crap. You just like her and can't see the bigger picture. All my damn life I've been dealing with whether I was black enough. I didn't ask for my circumstances but I got em. I get drug off from the country to the big ass money hungry city where the worst thing that happens is your cat accidentally gets ran over by a neighbor when they back out the driveway. I gotta face other brothers my age in this life looking down on me because I am privileged. Is it fair, naw. Is it a part of life, yes. Now, I gotta chance to understand and operate in an environment that I never was used too. That I never understood because all I saw was palm trees, sunshine and sunflowers. And you have the nerve to be upset that I am upset? I dunno what this means for you, but this is my life." I was pissed off to the highest degree of pistivity.

"Ramses, calm down. Trust me, you will do well with these youth in the centers and show them things."

"Skip the centers Mr. Lile. You don't see it. We meet them at these centers and send them right back to hell. And what do we get out of it? A pat on the back? Our ability to look in the mirror and smile? Let me ask you something Mr. Lile. When America goes to war, whether it be legit or under false pretense to rob a country blindly, do they go somewhere else to fight it? When they invaded Germany on D Day, did they launch on the beach in Mexico? The answer is no. They went to the source of the problem." He stood there quiet. I may have only been 16, but I was wise beyond my years.

"Mr. Lile?"

"Oh hush Ramses," he told me. "Look the fact is we are here. Do I feel bad for those kids? Yea. But I am not about to send a group of you all in harm's way to help out some shits who after we leave will fall right back into their own lil bullshit. They don't like us and frankly, I could care less. I'm here to smile, help and get out of dodge. Now, if you wanna let your pro blackness get in the way of this, then fine. When you get grown, you can come back and go into Ensley, Hoover, Westside, North side, whatever part of Birmingham or any city you want and make change. I'm here to be Leonard Lile, not Martin Luther King." He turned around and walked back toward Ms. Dockery and the rest of the group. So much for the North Philly multiracial adopted kid and his love for people huh? They started to file into a building while I was just standing there upset at the world.

"C'mon man," Carlos said, as he came over, put his arm around me and we walked into the building. Once we got in, all eyes were on us as everyone was seated in a huge conference room, along with a bunch of other kids who I had no idea were.

"Well will you two be joining us?," Ms. Dockery said. We both went to take seats in the back.

"Ok you all. Before we start with anything, we will have a day to ourselves, to get to know each other, learn the history of the city and some other stuff. For the first part, we will watch a 45 minute video on the history of Birmingham and some of the plights the people of the inner city have faced."

The lights dimmed as all these group of teens sat there

looking at this giant projector. Carlos immediately began to play with his phone while I seriously homed in on what was about to be shown. I had researched this city before I even came. Much like the temple in which I call my body, I study everything that I put into it. This was no different. Birmingham was built on the blood of black people in general. It was founded in 1871, in the post civil war era. It had many names such as the "Magic City," which was due to its quick uprising as a city. When you look at Alabama, you think countrified, home grown, togetherness and many great terms. However, Alabama has a rich history that dwells into the dark side. For many years, blacks in Birmingham and Alabama in general suffered the hardships due to racial oppression. Hell, they even nicknamed the city "Bombingham" because of how black homes were bombed.

The Klan ran free in the South, hanging blacks from trees, beating them on sight and denying them the basics that whites were allowed to have. It's most famous incident was probably the bombing of the 16th street Baptist church, where four young, black girls perished when a bomb exploded inside the church. That incident might have started the desegregation of America through the Civil Rights Act of 1964, but the hate and discontent towards my people still existed.

I watched the film with anger in my heart. It was saddening to see the travesty my people had to go through. I saw from the early years how blacks made up half of Birmingham's industrial workforce, yet they had to live in the poorest of conditions. It made me cringe, but not as much as to what I would see about 30 minutes in. The modern day Birmingham was a wild west shootout zone. Every gang you could imagine was down here from the Bloods that originated in Cali to the GD's that started in The Motherland of Chicago. Young brothers waged war with each other over streets corners, blocks and neighborhoods. One thing always astounded me about gangbangin. I used to wonder why these young brothers were defending a turf that they didn't even own. I watched for years as white families in the affluent cities of Huntington Beach, Newport Beach, Laguna Hills and Dana Point would come together if something didn't seem right in their neighborhood. And for all intents and purposes they had every right to do so, seeing that more than 90% of them had investments in their own communities.

Now, when I look at us, I see us shooting our brothers for being on a block that we don't even own. The Arab's own the liquor store. The Koreans own the hair shop. We barely put any business into our own neighborhoods and we fail to change that. I swore that if I ever got rich, I would put as many blacks on my team as possible. It didn't have anything to do with taking over the world. It had more to do with giving my people a chance. I had a chance to see the better life. It was my duty to pass that life on to the next man if I ever had the chance.

The movie finished up and the next thing they did was break us off into groups with kids from different cities across America. There were four cities that were represented here at project R.E.B.O.R.N. Newport Beach, California. Stamford, Connecticut. Beverly Hills, California. Tualatin, Oregon. The crazy thing that I noticed with all of these kids from four different cities were that me and Carlos were the only blacks here.

"Man what the hell we got ourselves into?," Carlos whispered to me.

"I dunno bruh. I dunno." Finally, we were split up. 48 kids and four groups of 12. When it was all said and done, I felt even more out of place. The only good thing I had was that Mr. Lile was head over my group, even though we had got into it earlier. As we all sat in one giant circle, he jumped it off with the most unexpected thing ever.

"Introduce yourselves. Tell the group your name, where you are from and a little bit about yourself to the group. I'll have my guy Ramses start it off." He said that with the greatest of joy, but I know he was full of it. I stood up looking at all of these blue eyes gazing a hole through me. I ain't gone front, it was one blonde who could get it.

"Hey y'all. My name is Ramses. I'm from Oklahoma City, Oklahoma, but relocated to Newport Beach when I was eight. I play football, love to read and I'm here to make the best out of this experience." A girl raised her hand.

"Why is your name Ramses? Kinda ghetto isn't it?" Excuse my French, but I wanted to slap this bitch into the next century with that lil smart ass remark. However, I had to remember to let the negative talk. They only hurt themselves and responding to ignorance in an ignorant matter just makes me look like I am the most ignorant one. So I responded with something so classic that I am pretty sure God called all the angels around and ceased judging folks at the pearly gates for a good minute.

"Well........miss. It's actually not ghetto. It's a reference to the Pharaoh Ramses the First, the great ruler of the 19th dynasty of Egypt. See my mom named me not to be stereotyped into what you think is a ghetto name. She, however, named me because she knew I would leave a legacy. See after Ramses, 11 more of his name would rule in Ancient Egypt, each leaving their mark. See miss lady, I am the beginning of greatness. I know the name may take you away from what you are accustomed to, but if you actually look at your name in the history text, maybe you could see that you maybe, just maybe you might be of some higher importance. Now, if you don't mind me asking you. What is your name?" She sat there silent for a minute as did every student, with their eyes gazed upon her.

"Umm.....my name is simply Cleo." I began to chuckle.

"What's so funny?," she asked.

"Well, what's funny is that you made a big deal about my name and you don't even know what yours means. See if you really dig deep, you were probably named after Cleopatra of Ancient Egypt, but I'll let you figure that out. Moral of the story is this. Don't assume one's character by a name. Now folks, that's my introduction." I sat down and everyone just remained quiet. All they needed was some Kermit tea and it would've been perfect.

"So ummm.....you over there. You're next." Mr. Lile pointed to some random guy who you could tell was nervous to follow up with what I had just said. I never said that to intimidate the crowd. I only stated it because it was factual and she, and everyone else needed to hear that. It was already bad enough that it felt like 2 vs. 46. I didn't need any more stereotypical BS thrown my way. As we finished our introductions, we got placed one on one with another individual from the group to begin the process of learning how to interact with someone different who was from another world. In truth, we were all from the same world I imagined. We all had on nice shoes, clothes, some even had on thousand dollar watches. Our worlds weren't different when you compared us by the amount of opportunity we had.

"Ramses man?"

"Ihmotep." As we shook hands, I kind of leaned back in my chair. "Ihmotep? That's dope man." He cracked a smile.

"It's good to know that someone likes it. I'm white and Egyptian. My dad, he married my Egyptian mother after he met her in Portland. I got most of his features, so to the naked eye, I look like I'm 100% Caucasian. However, your story man made me become proud of who I was. I was made fun of so much coming up because of my name. Kids didn't understand and neither did I. But the crazy part is that when we would see a minority in our neighborhood, there were some people who got real nervous. We had this Muslim kid who went to my junior high school that everyone called "Bomber" and I knew it hurt. See they knew me to just have a strange name, never knowing that I was half Egyptian, because I took on so many of my dad's features. It sucks when I see kids go through it based on their color or creed. It ain't right."

I totally dug this dude. He could relate to me and we listened for understanding of each other's situation. As our conversation progressed, he cut loose and told me the story of how he came to be. His dad was a Portland realtor who lived off his rewards in the city of Tualatin. Heading towards Washington Square one day, he stopped at a favorite restaurant of his. When the waitress came, he said his dad claimed to see the most beautiful site of his life. She was different, kind and seemed like she had everything going for herself. Come to find out, she didn't have everything going for herself. In a city that is 80% white, she faced hurdles at times. She was barely making ends meet. To put it plain and simple, his mom didn't have a car. She took the bus to work. From the first date, she informed him of her hardships and his heart instantly became open. Did he give her the world, no. He simply allowed her inside of his life to provide him balance. He helped her achieve her goals in life and she helped him become a much calmer man who used discernment more than ever when it came to dealing with everyday life and people. Long story short, he was born in only their second year together. I could dig it. I told him my story and he was instantly awestruck. As we winded down the 30 minutes we were allotted, we were stopped by Ms. Dockery.

"Ok group, I hope you are accustomed to the person you are with. This is the same person you will be staying with when you are placed in these homes and go out to do your missions in the community. We will now break for lunch in the cafeteria that is down the hall. Enjoy yourselves and meet back in here at one o'clock so you can meet your families." While everyone else went to lunch, me and 'Tep' as I called him stayed choppin' it up, getting to know more about one another. This was gonna be the start of an empire I could tell. One o'clock came around faster than a shark that smelled blood in the ocean. We now had our bags that were taken off of the bus during lunch.

"Ramses and Andrew!" I turned and looked at him.

"Andrew?"

"I used my middle name dawg. I didn't wanna have to slap one of these white silver spoons in here." All I could do was laugh as we chucked our bags over our shoulders and made our way towards the door. When we stepped outside, we were greeted by a black family.

"How y'all doing? Fred Turner. This is my wife Megan Turner." We shook hands, put our bags in the car and we were on our way. The drive was nothing more than five maybe six minutes. When we pulled up to the house, it indeed looked like Magic City. It was a magical sight to see in this city. More so, it was magic to see one of our kind have what they have. We followed them inside this castle of a home. It was even bigger than the place I called home. The first thing I noticed was the monstrous chandelier sitting atop the ceiling and the winding stairwells. Tep's mouth was dropped while I was just in awe.

"Sir," I told him.

"When I think about the Southside of any city, I automatically think about poverty and despair. This has clearly changed my view about living on the Southside." He just laughed.

"Come in the living room boys. My wife will heat some food

up and I can tell you all about this Southside." We sat on an oversized plush sectional couch which was tan in color. If that wasn't enough, the 70" television looked like you could walk into it.

"You? Young man," Mr. Turner asked Tep.

"Huh?" That boy was so in tune with this house that he didn't even hear Mr. Turner ask him the question.

"So Ihmotep. Like the great priest and medicine man. Son, you truly don't know the greatness that lies within you."

"I'm honored to hear you say that sir, but I know greatness is much more than just a name."

"Indeed it is, but yours translate into the healer. So use that when we go on our journey tomorrow." As his wife brought out a pitcher of Kool aid, some plates and a huge bucket of seafood, Mr. Turner continued on.

"See all of those other kids; the folks they are with will probably take them to a youth home or the local boys' town. Have 'em talk to a few youngsters, make em feel good and then go back to sit on their fat rich asses. Me, nah. See, I didn't always have this. I'm from a section of B-ham called Ensley. We are hood. I am hood. I have just learned to turn the hood off to prosper in life. I read your profiles and were impressed. Not by the grades you made or what y'all do in y'all respective sports. Nah. I'm more impressed that y'all black and making it where you are making it. You have to remember one thing. We all struggle. The black raised in the projects struggles for survival and the thought of making it out. The black raised in the majority white burbs struggles to fit in and be accepted by his culture. None is greater than the other, because they are both a struggle that has to be dealt with accordingly." It sounded like déjà vu of my mindset. Fred was on it tonight. As we finished, he let us know what was about to go down.

"I want you two to rest up. Around 8 o'clock, we're headed

over to the projects where my family stays. I got cousins on the wrong side, but they respect me enough not to do their dirt around me. I told em I got two young men that I want them to break in and show them what life is like on the other side. Trust, it's nothing to fear. But in order to understand somebody's walk, you must first put your feet in their shoes and walk the path that they do daily. You boys make yourselves comfortable. Y'alls room is upstairs and to the left. If you need me, I'll be in my bedroom. See y'all tonight." As he left out leaving all this ocean goodness to me and Tep, we just looked at each other.

"You ready for this experience?," Tep asked me.

"Nah bruh. I'm ready for this transformation." We then just looked at each other. I think we were both hoping that we would simply survive. Not so much physically, but mentally.

2 THE OTHER SIDE OF THE TRAP

Journey to blind traps
take steps with good precision
you will leave out great

"Wake up boys! Let's go!" I arose at the sound of that loud voice to Mr. Turner in the doorway. He was dressed in all black, with a bulletproof vest on. On the side of his right hip, I saw a gun in a holster, so I knew that things were about to get real.

"Tep?! Tep?!" This dude was on the couch in the room knocked the hell out, not knowing what was going on.

"I got him," Mr. Turner said. He went over to Tep and un holstered his pistol.

"A boy?," he said. Tep opened his eyes and by the size of em, you could tell that his bladder was about to run. He slowly rose up with the pistol lined up perfectly to his forehead.

"Let's go son. I told you that tonight you gonna get broke in. You wanted this experience, then you are gonna get it." Tep was shaken to his core, as was I.

"Meet me in the driveway in ten minutes. Both of you." He turned around, walked out and I just stared at my boy.

"Man what the hell have we gotten into man?," Tep whispered to me.

"This crazy muthafucka got guns on him and shit. Man we bout as good as dead."

"Calm down man," I told him. "Look, I'm sure as hell ain't nothing gone happen to us bruh. He said we good. We just gotta man up and handle our business. Look bruh, I'm going into the unknown just like you. But like you, I ain't never seen this part of life, so I'm trying to understand it and get a better appreciation for what I got. We came to help folks, but we also came to learn about ourselves. I got you bruh. Trust me." Right then, Mr. Turner started honking his horn downstairs. It was time to roll out. We headed downstairs to see his wife by the door.

"Good luck y'all and see y'all tomorrow," she said. Boy if that wasn't something chilling to tell to a pair of sixteen year olds, I don't know what was. We walked out the door to this tinted out suburban. I hopped in the front and Tep hopped in the back seat. As soon as the door closed, we sped off into the night.

"Aight look boys. First things first. I'mma detective. So don't worry bout the guns, scanners, none of that. Matter fact, I'm sorry if I scared the shit outta y'all back there. Like I said, I got cousins and shit who still operate on the wrong side of the law. They respect me though like I said not to bring certain shit around me. However, tonight, I told 'em the situation. I told 'em what my plans were. I want y'all to see this shit. I don't know how these niggas gone react to you, but just know that I ain't gone let nothing happen to y'all. Aight?" I nodded my head as Fred looked in his rear view mirror.

"You got me Tep?"

"Yes sir," Tep said with an obvious lump in his throat. We eventually got away from the high price life and hit the freeway until things changed for real.

"Welcome to Ensley boys. This my old stomping grounds. Here, you'll find any and everything you need to know about life."

I looked out the tinted windows and seen what I hadn't seen ever. Cats were posted up in front of houses. The liquor store was illuminated as if it were the church of the community. I thought that was ironic. The liquor store was lit up but the church lights weren't on. We rolled through side streets, back alleys, the whole time me and Fred were engaging in convo about his life around here.

"So everyone must know your truck huh?"

"Yea they do. See I became the law, but I never became the law to them. You see all these niggas hanging out everywhere when we roll through. I can guarantee at least one of them was on their cell phones letting em know that

"Tommy T" was on the blocks.

"How'd you get that name?" That's when the story of stories came about.

The year was 2000, long before I was even in this teenage phase. A then 26 year old Fred Turner was fresh to the police force. He was over at his grandmother's house enjoying a family function with his cousins. To make a long story short, as him and a few of his cousins were relaxing on the porch, giving him playful shit about being a cop, a dark blue, tinted up Chevy Impala came hauling ass down the street. Someone from the back seat let out five shots from a measly 357.

The car sped off into the night. The shooter was so terrible that no one on the porch was hit. However, one bullet did hit an unintended target. His grandmother. He said he heard the screams from inside the house as his grandma lie on the floor fighting for her elderly life. She was in the kitchen whippin' up a batch of her famous cheddar biscuits that he said would've put red Lobster out of business. The fam bam called 911 and was desperately trying to stop her from bleeding to death. He said that by the time the ambulance arrived, he knew she was gone, even though they took her and tried to revive her. She was gone by the time she hit the hospital and it was all over for him as far as upholding the law as he was concerned.

He was now back to being the hood cat from the Westside of Birmingham who had to deal out street justice. Birmingham was a big city according to people in Alabama, but for the residents, it was small. Everyone knew everyone and it didn't take long to find someone when you needed them. At lil bit after two the next morning, him and his cousins loaded up the choppers, sweepers and anything else that fired off rounds. They went and roamed the streets looking for their target.

"That's the nigga house right there," one of his cousins said. His fam bam stopped the whip. Fred said at that point, him and three of his cousins got out. Rather than spray up the one house, they all spread out and on the same count, they lit up the night sky with round after round from the choppers. Killing one person wasn't in their mindset. Why shoot up a house when they can tag up the whole block? They did this until their guns were damn near empty and they all peeled back to the van and jetted out. No one saw them. No one could give a description of the vehicle. By the time the sun arose and the news had reported it, 12 people were dead including two children under the age of six. He was coined the nickname "Tommy T" by his fam because according to one of them, he looked like one of the old fashioned gangsters when he was shootin'. Back then, he had no regrets. The inner city nigga had taken over the man who was trying to keep his life on the straight and narrow.

I have to live with that every day for the rest of my life. It wasn't so much the act of shooting. It's what the act of shooting caused. Grief. I killed two kids. A grown ass man killing two innocent youth who didn't have a chance to grow up. I live with that all day and night. I try not to let it bother me, but when I roll up on the scene of a young man or lady murdered, I flash back to it. It's hard at times I tell you. It's hard." Suddenly, we came to a stop.

"Aight boys, what's about to happen next, don't be alarmed." Out of nowhere the truck doors opened with guns in our faces.

"Put these bags over y'all heads, shut up and let's roll. Waddup famo." The next thing I remember was all black. We were led into a house or building nearby, which was obvious because of the steps we had to walk up and down. We were sat down. Tep at this point was breathing deep, nervous as all get out.

"Calm ya ass down man. Ain't no one gone hurt you." The hoods came off and it looked like something out of a Taliban video. The room was lit in an eerie blue light. I saw cats with masks on and guns in their hands. Against the wall, sitting down, there was a brother with dreads and golds who was just smiling at us with the most evil grin you could imagine.

"Yo lil bright and damn near white. Tell me your story." Tep was frozen solid and really didn't know what to say.

"Hello man. You want my gun? Make you feel a lil more comfortable." The sweat was pouring down this boy's head like he had played four quarters in a NBA game.

"Nah, nah," Tep said in his muffled voice.

"I'm half white, half Egyptian, so that's why I got a lil tint on me. Man, I just wanna know what it's like. I never seen nothing like this." Ol' dude smiled that evil smile once again.

"Don't be nervous mane. We ain't here to hurt you. We could, but this ain't what this about. You see my mans who brought you, he famo. He was this before he became that," pointing at his badge hanging on his waist.

"I already know why you here. I know why your mans is here. Trust, everything that the eyes see ain't truth. We wanna understand you as well. You, nigga who a pharaoh. Tell me your story."

"You got a square?," I asked him.

"Ol boy looked around at his goons and turned back to me.

"Well, well. I see Oklahoma still in you. A Raji, give my mans a square." I didn't smoke, but in my mind, I thought it would ease some of the tension in the room, which would make things easier for Tep. His man's handed me one and lit it for me. As I blew out the first puff, I let it all hang out.

"All my life, since my mama and daddy died, then my uncle, I been living in a lie. See every brother I meet thinks I'm just this kid who has had the greatest of lives. They think I ain't black. They think by me living where I live, I ain't got no love for them. Truth is, I just wanna be normal. All the glitz and glam ain't for me. It's what I have become accustomed to due to the circumstances, but I'm human man. I'm black like everyone in this room. I get tired of cats when they see me say you ain't one of us. Roll out or get rolled up. I ain't come on this earth to have to fight for acceptance from my own peoples." The room stood still and nobody made a noise.

"A Tommy T, hand lil nigga that brick over there." Fred walked over to a table while lookin' at me, giving me a grin. He grabbed a plastic wrapped brick of what I assumed was coke off the table and threw it at me. I caught it and really didn't comprehend what I was holding in my hand. I had never seen nothing like this in person, but I was more so trying to understand why he gave this to me.

"Right there fam. You got over $40,000 in yo hands. Pure, uncut, grade A white bitch."

"But what's the point of you letting me hold this?" Again that evil grin came across his face. I swear he looked like a gremlin when he did that.

"Raji. Hand him Tina." Suddenly the biggest dude in the room came over and handed me a gun I ain't never seen in my life. This bitch was heavy as all to be damned.

"Right there. You holding a custom made grenade launcher. I call her ass Tina because she makes whatever it hits sing. And like her songs, it's fire. See you wondering why I'm showing you this. It's so you can know what our life is like. You seen these streets on the way here. You struggle with your own accepting you. We struggling to make a way so we can eat. You think we wanna do this shit?," he asked as he raised up out the chair.

"Hell nah! We'd give our left nutsack to be able to live freely every day. But we can't. We stuck. So we gotta do what we gotta do to survive. A fam, bag they heads back up. We gone take y'all for a ride." *Here we go again* I thought. This car ride seemed longer than usual. I didn't even know what time it was or had an idea of where we were going. If I could estimate, we were riding for at least 45 minutes. The car all of a sudden came to a stop. The bag got pulled off my head.

"Get ya ass out," big Raji said. I got out to see we were in an abandoned field in the middle of God knows where. What I did notice besides this was that Fred and Tep were nowhere here with me. I was too scared to ask in fear of something going down, even though Fred said I was gravy.

"Walk over here mane. By the way, they call me Gold Mouth." I obliged without hesitation as I was followed by his four goons in which I only knew one of their names. We stopped at what seemed to be an open trench.

"See famo took ya mans back. He wasn't ready for this kinda stuff. But you, I gotta show you. Look in there." I walked up slowly to the edge and looked in. There in it lie a dead body. Ol' dude couldn't have been deceased anymore than a day or two, seeing how everything was still fresh.

"This the other side of the trap youngin. Newport will never show you this. Now why you think I brought you here?"

"I dunno," I responded.

"It's simple famo. This ain't you, so I want you to see this and never strive to be like us. We killers. Cold blooded killers. The only thing that's guaranteed is that none of us will ever see heaven. I just ask that when you get to that muthafucka you send me a postcard." He laughed his evil laugh and dapped me up.

"Let's go mane." The ride back was long and black, seeing that the bag was over my head once again. After about a 30 minute drive, we stopped. The bag was taken off and I saw Fred waiting for me.

"I got him from here famo." I nodded my head up to Gold Mouth and the crew as he smiled that smile and sped off into the night.

"Fred what time is it."

"It's a lil after two in the morning. The same time it was when I murked the block many years back. C'mon, let's go to the house and get some sleep." As we headed back to the glamour life, I had to ask him.

"So what happened with Tep?" Fred just let out a sigh.

"You know, and I ain't knocking him for it, but the experience of never seeing anything so tragic in life has him shook. I mean, he is literally ready to get on the plane and go home. He wants to understand every aspect, but he is not willing to face it. So the fam bam called me and I got him up outta there while you went on your way. So what did you see?" I just remained quiet, but it was obvious that he knew that I was hiding something.

"You saw a dead body. I already know. Thing is, it wasn't their work. It was one of their partnas. They kept a cool head round you. While you were in the basement amazed at bricks of coke, a text came through to one of them saying that they found "Peanut" body. Peanut was one of their runners and from round the hood. I allowed Gold Mouth to head out there to confirm it was him. That's why they took you to be all honest. Tomorrow morning it'll be a million cops over there, as I'll drop some lingo of I got a lead on the whereabouts. The game is screwed up, so be glad you don't have to see this on a night out and night in basis. Growing up here, it's like being in a bucket. The minute you try to crawl out, here comes another crab taking you back down, not letting you go anywhere. Eventually, you won't be able to crawl up out the bucket 'cause you'll be a stiff on the side of the road. This only a lil bit of what I'm a show you. Trust, it ain't the black experience, but since the experience consist of a lot of blacks, then it's only fair. You ever watch your shadow disappear in the dark?" I didn't get this question to be quite honest but I responded with a tiresome yeah. That's when he hit me with black knowledge bomb #9457.

"Whenever there is enough light, your shadow stays by your side. It can hang from ya feet at all different angles, but it still stays right by you. Then, when you enter into darkness, it disappears, leaving you alone to face obscurity. Well, that's how the hood is. One minute you on top of the world. Everyone around you is a bunch of shadows. The next thing you know, BOOM! You catch a charge and all those shadows disappear without a trace. All them niggas yo' day one niggas until it's time to do time with you. All them niggas are yo' day one niggas until it's time to join you in the cemetery. All them niggas is yo' day one niggas til someone like me get in their face and they start singing louder than Aretha and slaughtering your name worse than Drake did Meek. If you don't remember anything else, remember this. Your shadow isn't loyal. Rather look in the side mirror and tell me what it says?"

"The objects in the mirror are closer than they appear."

"You right. Those niggas are always closer than they appear to be. In truth, they are far off in the distance." That last sentence kept ringing in my head as we pulled up to the house. Those niggas are always closer than they appear to be. In truth, they are far off in the distance. I got out the car and walked in behind him, heading straight upstairs to the room. I entered in and saw Tep knocked out on the big ol' oversized couch that looked more comfortable than the actual king size joint that was in the room.

"Tep," I whispered as I shook him. "Tep? Tep?" He turned around all groggy.

"Sup dawg."

"Man what happened," I asked him. He slowly rose up as I took a seat and he wiped the boogers out of his eye.

"Bruh, I have never been so shook in my whole entire life. I mean, I thought I was ready to see what the other side was like. I was damn near having an asthma attack and I don't even have asthma. When I thought the night was over, I realized it was just the beginning." I looked at him kind of strange. I figured he had just been driven back to the house after everything was all said and finished. I quickly found out that wasn't the case.

"Bruh, so I'm in the car with Fred and he making sure I'm cool. I'm saying I am, but deep down, I know I was screwed up. He took me to a lil 24 hour eating joint real quick to get some grub. I thought everything was gravy by now. I had food in me and I was calm. I had my nerves back. Once we left, he took me on a drive. I didn't know where he was going. All I remember was him telling me that when you can't handle one situation, you sometimes have to go back in the past to face the present, and that will prepare you for the future. It's like dude is a modern day philosopher or some shit. He took me to the block that he shot up all those years ago. For me, it was something I couldn't describe. Like dawg, we were literally in the hood. The rivals hood where he put in work.

Fred loaded up two guns and got out the car, leaving it running. When he got to my side, he knocked on the window, signaling for me to let it down. I let it down and he asked me something. What was it like when they used to see your mother wasn't what they wanted her to be? I couldn't comprehend what he was asking me so I asked him to say it again. What was it like for her being tanned skin in a city where that ain't common?

At that moment, I could only think about the worst thing I ever saw. My mom's got punched at the store when I was six. I was in there with her. It was two bald headed white dudes. My mother dropped and they just stared at me. Lil mixed bitch! was what one of them said as he then spit in my face. I mean literally, this dude dropped a pool size hawk of spit right in the middle of my face. I told him, it wasn't easy for her. Right then he shook his head. He said this wasn't easy for him, because when he was shooting, he remember the red house with the single window in the front. He pointed to it and said right when he aimed that way, a lil girl peeked her head through the curtain. It was an adrenaline rush combined with little time as he saw her, but didn't see her. Once the bullet went through the window, he didn't come back to reality until they were back on the freeway headed back to his grandma's house. Then, he got back in the car, stared at me for about five seconds and we hauled ass up outta there and back to the crib."

"What did you take from that?," I asked him.

"I took exactly what he wanted me to take from it. You have to face fear to get past fear. And truthfully, the worst fear we have is with our own selves and our own wrong doings." I had looked at things from many different angles, but never that one. Some knowledge and science had been dropped on me deep. I ended the convo with Tep, letting him get back to sleep. As I literally threw my clothes on the floor and prepped to get in the bed, I noticed a frame above the bed. From the lil light I had in the room, I saw it was one of Fred's degrees from the Freemasons. It was no wonder why dude was so intellectual and a science dropper. People feared what they didn't understand. With him representing that /G\ and that compass, I now understood his logic. I plopped down into bed and let my mind wonder about a few hours from now until I fell asleep.

"Breakfast is ready you guys" that was Fred's wife waking us up around nine o'clock. I was still a lil tired, but some food and coffee would wake me up in an instant. Yea I know. Drinking coffee at sixteen probably had me in old man status. We chilled in the living room, Tep and I, flippin' through the channels until we caught the morning news. There it was as plain as day. The site where Gold Mouth took me. The body had been discovered and the live feed was coming from the help that was flying above it. I didn't tell Tep I had been there, seeing that he may freak the hell out. He literally looked like he had seen a ghost. As we continued watching, my phone rang. It was my mom. We talked for a good fifteen minutes. She wasn't worried, but when she became inquisitive, I made up a lie so smooth that you would've thought I pimped a cucumber into a pickle with a carrot. As I got off the phone, I wanted to get up out of here and see this neighborhood.

"Mrs. Turner?"

"Yes," as she came out the kitchen wiping her hands.

"Is there anywhere around here we can go while we wait for your husband to come home?"

"It's a basketball court out back if y'all wanna head out there." Tep heard that and literally broke his neck going out the door. He loved basketball and was a star in Oregon. I followed behind and walked outside behind him.

"AHHH! Lamarcus Aldridge style boy!" All I could do was laugh. Dude had been quiet for the longest, but you put a basketball in his hands and all of a sudden he turned into the great light, almost white hope.

"Let's get this game of horse going man?," he asked. I obliged and we started to shoot.

"How you think them other kids doing Tep?"

"Man, if it's anything like what we experienced, they probably boo booin bricks. However, I ain't see no other black folks at the center when we were out there, so they probably at a community center talking to 5th graders or some nonsense like that." We did this for the next hour until Fred came back to the house and joined us out back.

"Y'all good?!"

"Yes sir," we said in unison.

"Good, cause now round 2 starts. Let's jump in the truck." Before we did, Tep raised his hand.

"Naw Tep. It ain't gone be like last night. Its daytime and I got something else planned for you. It's never the same thing twice. C'mon. you good." You could feel the tension rise off of his body as he headed back in the house. We got in the truck and headed out. This time, he showed us a few sights. We passed UAB or the University of Alabama Birmingham for those who may not know. He showed us spots where King marched and many civil rights activists gathered at back in the day to protest the injustice that they faced in the Deep South. Then, there it was. The 16th street Baptist church. Fred parked the car and told us to get out. We were here where bloody history took place. I closed my eyes for a minute and tried to envision what it was like that fateful day. I saw nothing but fire and heard screams of agony. I thank God for what I have because I am not sure if I could have survived in those times.

"You see this here boys. This is what you come for. This is the black that you need to see. Guarantee, all those other kids aint seeing this. Those white folks ain't gone bring 'em nowhere near this. They gone keep 'em in the schools and community centers to give them a pat on the back and call it a day. They think they are enhancing these kids when in truth; they aren't doing anything for them. How you gone help the poor if you don't go where the poor are? How you gone understand hood politics if you never talk to hood people or walk in their shoes. That's what last night was about. It gave y'all a chance to walk in someone else's shoes so you could understand. Was it the best example? No. However, it was a realistic example. The one thing I want y'all to take away from here in about a week and a half is that you cannot escape reality. You can dream about better days all you want. The fact is there are poor folks. There are those who are still in poverty. There are those who are mentally challenged. In order to help them, you must face them. Let's go."

We walked back to the car with a new understanding on not just people, but on life. We peeled out until we arrived downtown at the headquarters for the Birmingham Police. Man, I had seen this on First 48 so many times, but now I was actually here. We walked in to the looks from the fellow officers. There were no awkward stares. If you seen one black teenager, then you seen em all. Fred went and dapped up on of his co workers.

"A y'all wait over there in those chairs. I'll be done in like 5-10 minutes." I had never in my life been in a police station, let alone spent extended time in one. Me and Tep made small conversation while waiting to pass the time by. With every phone ring I heard, I thought they were on their way to another case of murder or robbery. It was just my imagination running wild, as I was trying to put myself in their shoes.

"Aight, y'all ready? Follow me." We were ready as we were ever gonna be as we followed him and another guard back past all the doors to what seemed like hell itself. After the metal detectors, the searches, all that, we were nearing the cell block area. Fred stopped us before we went in.

"Lemme tell y'all something. I just talked to you about facing fear. I got a cousin who is waiting for transport for triple murder in here. He wanna holla at y'all. It's gone be a guard in there with y'all and I'll be outside. He fam, like blood fam, so I don't see anything poppin' off, but I gotta take precautions." Tep raised his hand again.

"You couldn't bring him to the white room or whatever it's called?" Fred just laughed.

"Do you wanna learn about your own or are you gonna run away from the negative all of your life." He was quiet, not saying a word. Fred then looked at me.

"Are you gonna back out?"

"Hell nah," I told him. He looked at the other officer and smiled.

"My man. Let's roll." The sounds coming from behind those doors were music that I never wanted to my ears. We walked down this long hall of nothing but small glass panes on doors until we got to the end. When the door was opened, I seen the biggest negro I had ever seen in my 16 years of life. Just imagine Michael Clarke Duncan mixed with CT Fletcher. Whatever this dude momma had fed him as a youngster had obviously paid off. I swear it looked like he had been eating whole human beings his entire life.

"STAX," Fred called out to him.

"Tommy T. My blood. My family. My nigga." They shook up and hugged. You could tell this ain't where he wanted to be, but the streets called and he had to perform street justice.

"I got two lil partners who I'm trying to teach some life

lessons too. They ain't accustomed to this life. All they know is streets of gold and palm trees. Help 'em understand what it's like on the other side. They good kids who been put through hell by their own because they're privileged. Again, help 'em understand." STAX turned that big burly neck over to look at both of us.

"Aight. Sit down in these two chairs youngins. I been waiting for y'all." Fred went outside and the other officer posted up in the corner. He was a brother too, but it looked like he knew STAX and what he was about so he didn't stand with any anticipation of anything.

"What's yo name mane?"

"Ramses."

"Ramses," as he snapped his head back. "Like the pharaoh right?"

"Yea that be me."

"I dig it man. What's yours lite bright?"

"Drew is what I go by, but my real name is Ihmotep. I don't like to tell nobody because it starts a lot of my parents are looney type biz." STAX just stared at him. "What you mixed with?"

"White and Egyptian sir."

"Well lemme tell you one thing. You got more black blood in you than a lil bit. Don't you ever be ashamed to be proud of your heritage. I don't care how many white folks you grew up around. Hell they name their kids after Vikings, Scotts, all that shit. Embrace yours! Because its yours! You understand?!" I aint gone lie, that you understand he said sounded like it punched a hole in my chest.

"Yes sir," Tep responded.

"Look, I know why y'all here. My cousin already put me on game. This ain't about whether or not you black. Its about seeing the real black. The real black is both of you. I ain't a representation of us. Oh sure, they throw the videos on television with the stupid shows and make you think that we are all ignorant. That ain't us. I'm in here simply because of bad choices. I'm a gangster by nature. GD. Gangster Disciple. 7-4 'til the world blow. I got more bodies under my belt than Mike Tyson in his prime. I ain't preaching this because I'm proud. I'm preaching this because I want y'all both to know exactly who you dealing with. This is me, but this ain't our race. Its easy for me to sit up here and say that I woulda traded my left nut to grow up like y'all, but I'd be lying. Poverty made me what I am. Naw, scratch that. I made me who I am. Lemme tell y'all something and I hope this sinks into y'all thick ass skulls. Don't ever blame your environment for what you are. It may have an influence on you, but it doesn't make you who you are. Some of the world's best doctors, lawyers, all that shit come from the projects. And some of your worse drug dealers and scam artists come from the affluent neighborhoods of America. You gone be judged and you can't avoid that shit. You can however choose to be what you want to be. Its yo' life. Don't be me. I'm on my way to death row possibly. And you know what, I could care less. I chose this life. But just cause I chose this life, don't mean that I'm gonna influence the next generation to choose it as well. Every man is responsible for his own destiny. Y'all chose."

The fire in his speech was evident by the sweat that ran down off his bald head as he talked. Me and Tep were left speechless. Here was a hardened criminal, who at the same time showed that he had care in his heart. Lesson #9687 about being black. Mistakes only make you a bad person if you influence the next brother man to do the same thing you did. Being gangsta wasn't about the bodies you lay in wake. Being gangsta was simply about being about your life in a positive way. Tep shook up with STAX and walked out. As I dapped up with him, he pulled me close to him.

"You chosen," he whispered in my ear. With a head nod

respectively both ways, I walked out. I don't know if my name was now Lucious Lyons, but the empire that I dreamed of started to build inside of me.

We made our way back to the center on the South side where we had all met on our initial departure. While we were walking in as if we had a for sure certain mind shift, I noticed the other kids were going about things as if nothing had even happened. I saw one of my classmates Ryan and talked to him for a good minute. He said that he and another kid from Beverly Hills had been taken into a home and did nothing but Skype visits with underprivileged youth in another part of the state. Besides that, he says the folks he was living with took him shopping, buying him all sorts of things. Deep down, I was angered. As crazy and trife as Mr. Lile sounded, I realized it wasn't just him. These adults didn't give a damn about the poor. All they cared about was creating the illusion that they were doing something. With the adults in a whole 'nother section of the building, it was just us. It was too much for me as I really felt that God's wrath was about to pour down something serious on someone. It wasn't right and it wasn't fair. I texted my mom.

"Never again." I didn't get a text back within ten minutes, so I assumed that she was out on a nature walk or something, because she absolutely loved doing that. It was literally me and Tep. Black was here for black and everyone else was just present. They didn't care about us, nor what we went through. It was almost like I was four again, and for the next two years, I was with my Uncle Ronnie. All of these kids were Uncle Ronnie. They ain't give two cares in the world. It was ok. I had something for their asses.

Nighttime rolled around and the neighborhood was pretty quiet. There was a ladder that was attached to my room window just in case of fire. Mr. Taylor always kept his bicycle on the side of the house. If they wanted to know how we felt as a people, they for damn sure was about to feel the wrath of 400 years. Whether it be Black Wall Street or even way back to the Haitian revolt of 1791, they were gonna feel it. I snuck off on his bike with a lighter in my pocket and a black rag. Before I grabbed either, I was smart enough to shave my arms with my clippers, shower and put on latex gloves. I threw on a long sleeved shirt that I had, ensuring that I wiped off any loose fibers with a lint brush. I biked it all the way to the center where we had gathered and went around the back. As I prepared to put my plan into play, I noticed a camera that was pointed directly at me. Damn, I thought. I came back around to the front to see a security guard.

"Hey you!" I stopped dead in my tracks as I seen the gun raised at me. I put my hands up immediately.

"What are you doing back there?!" My immediate response had to be dead on. This was Alabama and you know folks were itchin' to pull a trigger to kill a black man.

"I'm part of the group who is here on the project to help the less fortunate. I'm from California, so I never knew what it was like to ride a bike with a crisp, official springtime breeze. I apologize if I trespassed. I only biked where I knew where I was going." I was hoping like hell that he would buy that.

"What do you have on gloves for?!," the gun steady pointed at me. Again, my quick thinking came into play.

"I'm a germophobe sir. This is my sponsors bike and I have no clue who has been riding this thing. Excuse my city talk, but I don't know what's down here in the country." He walked up on me slowly, footstep by footstep. He stopped about three paces in front of me. I had never looked down the barrel of a gun. What I saw was a black hole that said to me I am ready to consume your soul.

"AAAcho!!!" I sneezed and looked back at him.

"C-c-c-can you pull my rag out of my pocket sir and wipe my nose?" His eyes squinted a little bit as he lowered the gun.

"Well you really are a germaphobe I see." With a smile and a laugh, he said ok. As I wiped my nose, he told me to just be mindful next time because he didn't want to mistake me for someone trying to bring harm to the community. With a yes sir and a handshake, he let me go on my way. As I was riding back, I really thought to myself,

"What in the good hell was I thinking?" I was really about to start a fire and burn some of their stuff down. Even crazier, I was about to be the next black man on the news shot dead by a white man. But what good would that have done had I succeeded on my mission? It would've only been a temporary victory, but it could never replace the burning that took place in the 1950's and 60's. I thought about all the images that I seen on that video we watched before we got placed with our families. The fires, the dogs, the water hoses, the hangings, the beatings, etc. It was hard to bare. I actually started to cry as I rode this bike. I was not feeling what it was like to be Black in America. The illusion I had couldn't even compare to the reality that a lot of my people were facing. The cycle continued. Everything was just done in a different way.

I stopped the bike directly in front of the house and walked out back to look at the stars. I wondered how many of them were the dead souls of black folks who died just so I could have an attempt to make it in this cruel and unjust world. It was almost unbearable. Suddenly, a hand touched my shoulder and damn near scared the bejeesus out of me.

"Oh Mrs. Taylor. I apologize. I was just out here clearing my head and you scared me." She simply kept her hand in place and looked up with me.

"They are there. I know what you are thinking. How many dead souls did it take for us to be where we are today." I turned around and looked at her with a shocked look on my face. "Trust me, I know. A kid of your caliber just doesn't look at stars without a purpose. One of those is my great grandmother, Annie May Hathaway. It was way back in the 1950's AND 60's when the Klan was marching through Birmingham. Oh my grandmother was strong. Y'all think these Bloods and Crips are gangstas. They ain't have a damn thing on her. She could scare the piss out of any and everybody except for Jesus Christ himself. Anywho, the Klan marching through the city was just one opposition she faced. It wasn't until 1963 that she became etched in Alabama lore. It was eight days in hell from what the old folks told me. I mean, to them, everyday was hell living in Birmingham, Alabama.

For eight straight days, however, the devil was sitting front row to witness something even he would cringe at. It was jumped off by an old man they called "Bull." Racist wasn't the word to describe him. A Klansman is racist. A skinhead is racist. Donald trump is racist. From what I was told, this man would even make them scratch their heads. In 1963, after years of bus boycotts orchestrated by King, "Project C," what they called it, took effect. That C supposedly stood for confrontation. In the eyes of the white man, it stood for colored, coons or whatever BS they wanted to come up with. On May 2, it all jumped off. Kids all of ages started to march the streets and in return, they were met with firehouses, nightsticks and most sickening of all, dogs. What kind of human being would attack another human being with a dog? I'll tell you who. A human who is not a human at all. Once this raged on, the term turnt up as you youngsters say came into effect.

Everybody had now come out in full force and Annie May was one of them. From what I have been told by a lot of old heads, My granny was fighting a cop and a dog at the same time. The cop was swingin' on her, but she was giving haymakers to him and that rat ass smelling mutt of his. It took about five cops to subdue her in the end. Once the smoke cleared, however, my granny may have had blood on her face, but those PO-Lease-men, which ain't nothing but humans leased out to mess with po' people, felt the wrath of her. There little baby, doggie, mutt or whatever you wanna call his ass lost his eye permanently. She witnessed hell her whole life, but that day, along with the other seven days, were some that stayed in her cranial for all time. My great grandmother died in 1984, on an August 16th day, but she forever lives on through me. What you gotta realize is this. Where you are at, you have to continue the fight. Don't let the fact that you are well off make you ever think that you can just leave your people behind. Help in some way, like you are doing now. It's cool that you are here. You are still a teenager, however. Just make sure that this experience carries with you when you become a full fledged adult. Trust me, the time is coming. The hatred, the disdain for your skin tone, it's coming. It may not be shown directly. It may have already been shown a little bit. Just know it's coming though on a whole 'nother level that you have never seen. It will be when you least expect it." She gave me a kiss on the cheek.

"Goodnight. And oh yea, Fred flips out about his bike. I saw you take off on it. I just prayed you made it back before he saw you." She walked in the house and I sat there with the stars above me. I pulled out that cloth and lighter, and just stared at it for a good minute. I was really about to flame something up. But what would that have done? It could've got me thrown in prison and I would never have the chance to reach out to someone who may need my guidance in the future. Lesson #9698 of being black. Always be the mental man before you become the physical man. Pain will give a person a memory of what not to do anymore, that is true. However, if you attack the mind, a scar will resonate to which no healing can ever occur from. You ever see those soldiers who come back from war in Iraq and Afghan who don't have any war wounds on the outside, but are mentally tore up inside of their skull? That's what I am talking about. The mind is more powerful than we all think. You destroy the mind of the opposition and the rest of their body will fall.

Morning came and everything seemed lined up for greatness today. I heard birds singing and the sun was breaking through the clouds enough that you would think nothing but happiness and joy was occurring. I started to think about the old white dude with the 'fro who used to paint on PBS. He always talked about "Happy Trees." Everything just felt right today. "A man, what we on today you know," Tep asked.

"Hell if I know bruh." We were still lying in our room, having the television look at us instead of the other way around. The door came open and Mr. Taylor came in with an ecstatic look on his face.

"You boys wanna go out and eat breakfast? I'm off today."

"Good with me," Tep said, raising up and getting crunk at the thought of eating some food. I jumped up myself and hopped in the shower, feeling that today would be a day of awesomeness. It was Friday and the weekend was here. Sure, it wasn't one where I would be going to the beach or anything like that, but it felt just as important. I finished up, threw on my clothes for the day and headed downstairs, where Tep and the Taylor's were having what seemed like a funny convo.

"What y'all laughing about?," I asked 'em.

"Nothing man. Just some wildness about sports. He talking about I'm the next Blake Griffin and Steph Curry. You know us light skinned brothers are taking over." I did laugh at that, 'cause I mean, dude was right. Curry and Klay beat Lebron and Kyrie in the finals. Drake destroyed Meek Mill. Michael killed Morris in The Perfect Man movie. Yea, light skinned had made a come up in some recent years I agree.

"C'mon y'all. Let's roll. You coming with us lovely?" Mrs. Taylor shook her head no and we went on about our way.

"So where we going Mr. Taylor?," as we all entered the truck.

"I can't tell you right now. It's more than breakfast." We peeled out like usual and hit up McDonald's drive thru.

"Man I thought we were going to breakfast sir?," Tep said.

"Gimme nine Egg McMuffin sandwiches. Eat on the go boy. That's how we doing it today. You want me to order some more?" I knew then it was about to be day three of madness. We left the drive thru smashing like never before. I didn't know where we were going, but hitting freeway 280 North, I just knew it was another journey down memory lane for Fred. I was thinking to myself do I really have to put another bag over my head. After about ten minutes more on the road, the journey winded down...at a big ass stadium. What we were doing here, I had no clue. That was until we pulled up near the bus and I saw some of the kids from the initial meet and greet, including Carlos.

"Waddup mane," as he came up to the whip dappin' me up.

"Bruh, what in the world are we doing here?" That's when Carlos hit me with it.

"Oh you aint hear bruh? Between us, Beverly, Tualatin and Stamford, its 19 of us that play football. Guess who we about to scrimmage today in a 7 on 7?" My mind was shocked beyond belief. It's only one team that you think of when you think about Alabama High School Football. That was Hoover High School. They were located here in Hoover, Alabama. The mighty Orange and Black attack of the Buccaneers. They have been to the state finals 17 times and brought back the 'ship 11 times. When you think of high school football in the state of Alabama, you think about these boys. In Cali, we were flashy, up tempo, more of the Hollywood style of breaking you with speed. Down here, they had it all. Speed, strength and just the knack to hit you in the mouth. I thought coming to Birmingham was the biggest challenge during my two weeks. Being a premiere football player, however, this turned out to be the biggest and baddest challenge that I least expected.

SEC boys versus a Big Ten worshipper. Born in Big 12 country but raised in Pac 12 country. Yea, it's kinda odd how all that played out. I wanted to play for Sparty and crew while growing up as a USC fan. I guess it was that green and white that had me hype to play for 'em. Not to mention the white out game against Michigan many moons ago when Peko returned that fumble for a touchdown. That is something that is etched in my memory bank for all time. I was known around Cali, but I wanted to take over the Midwest and all of college football as a whole. We walked into this monstrosity of a stadium. From the looks of it, you could tell that it easily seated a good 10,000. As the field came into view, some members of Hoover were in the middle of the field warming up. They had to be at least 30 deep. Also, in the middle of the field were several groups of adults who had brought us in for the two weeks we were slated to be down here. As we got closer, everything stopped and all the Hoover players turned towards us. The stare down continued as we got closer and closer to the sidelines.

"Bring it over," a man in a Crimson Tide hat yelled. We jogged it over to midfield where he stood in the middle of both groups. Oh boy, you would've thought World War 3 was about to start with the way they were looking at us.

"Okay now boys. You've got the best in the state of Alabama period. Versus the best from California, Connecticut and even a few from Duck and Beaver country up in Oregon. We're gonna get a good, clean, 7 on 7 scrimmage to tweak and peak everyone's skills. Plus, it gives us all a chance to interact and meet other people from other parts of the country. For you boys from out of town, we got all sizes of cleats out here too, so no worries about you slippin out here. Are there any questions?" That's when one of the Hoover players raised his hand.

"Yes there Rodney."

"Ain't no question coach. Rodney Stallings. All State wide receiver. 22 touchdowns last year. 94 receptions with 1,576 yards receiving. Headed to the greatest school. University of Alabama next year. The only university that matters 'round here or anywhere on this earth. All I wanna say is good luck cause y'all gone need it. This aint baby ball down here boys. This Alabama. 11 time state champs right here. 13 time national champs at the college level. **ROLL TIDE!** We the only team in Alabama that makes Orange look good, 'cause besides us, it's trash truck juice. But soon, y'all will be lunch meat just like Auburn." They got to high fivin' each other, and oohin and aahin. Everyone on our side was quiet. Me being me, however, I couldn't let that ride. I raised my hand.

"Yes sir Mr....what's ya name?"

"Ramses. Ramses Martin. Mr. All State linebacker and running back in California. 15 sacks, 164 tackles, 4 forced fumbles, 5 interceptions with one being a pick six. Lets not forget on offense either. 357 carries for 2,364 yards and 34 touchdowns. 41 receptions for 564 and 9 more touchdowns. Newport Harbor High School. Killing it on the California fields, but with Oklahoma roots. Born and raised for the first eight years of my life in Oklahoma, real football country. Boomer Sooner. 7 time national champs at the college level. Adrian Peterson. Brian Bosworth. Marcus Dupree. Big Tommie Harris. Lee Roy Selmon. Gerald McCoy. Hell I'll even throw in Jim Ross, the greatest announcer to ever live. I could go on partna. Headed to Michigan State after next year, because gang green looks better than crimson and a spartan damn sure goes harder than Dumbo the elephant." They started to rush forward as did me and a few of my other teammates. The adults got between us quick. Oh boy, we were about to get turnt up around these parts. They ain't like me disrespecting their mascot. Damn that. We were turnt up.

The Alabama National Guard, state police and any other emergency personnel had better get to this field as soon as possible. From how that went down, it was clear that tempers were about to flare and mouths were about to get bust wide open. Once the adults got everything under control, we split our teams into the best seven, with everyone else rotating in. We were on offense first. Carlos was out at wideout, where I knew he would maximize that 6'3, 210 pound frame on these scruff ass cornerbacks. Everyone else filled the positions, including a kid from Connecticut who was ranked in the ESPN top 100 for junior quarterbacks. Their defense lined up, barking and talking noise. I wasn't in the huddle for offense, but I already knew what was about to occur. Anything deep for Carlos. I know this ol' Alabamian wanted to test out his defense speed. The ball was snapped, ol' boy dropped back and I seen Carlos break off into a post pattern. However, when the ball should've been thrown, it wasn't. He lofted it late and the safety closed in.

"INTERCEPTION!," the old man yelled. The cat playing safety didn't even finish running to the end zone. He stopped after about ten steps and just launched the ball.

"THIS WHAT Y'ALL CALL FOOTBALL! Y'ALL BETTER LEAVE THAT BS IN THEM WACK STATES Y'ALL FROM!" My blood was now boiling as the defense had been called in. We were already lined up ready to go. Hoover broke their offensive huddle.

"I'M CROSSIN THE MIDDLE TRICK! STOP ME!" Ol' punk ass Rodney didn't know he was writing a check that his country ass couldn't cash. The ball was snapped. He ran that slant 'cross the middle just like he said. I ain't even wait for the ball to get to him. As soon as I seen it released, I clocked his ass with a right fist before it could even get to him. As he tried to get up, I cold clocked him again and then it was just one massive brawl. I can't remember who I was swingin' at, who I hit, who hit me or what. All I know is that by the end of it, adults were holding us back, we were separated and sent to different sidelines. Mr. Taylor pulled me away from the others.

"What the hell is wrong with you?!," as he grabbed my arm and walked me to the sidelines. Wiping the blood that was on my lip, I gave him the answer that he probably didn't wanna hear.

"Sir, he talked, I popped him, I popped him again and that's that. I ain't 'bout to let nobody think 'cause I'm from Newport Beach that I'm gone lay down like a bitch. I'm sorry I ain't from the hood or the country, but I'm still a brother." Mr. Turner's look didn't change, nor did his grip on my arm. After five seconds, he cracked a smile and whispered to me.

"That's what the hell I'm talking 'bout. Boy if you don't bring yo ass to Alabama after next year, I'm gone hunt you down myself." I smiled that bloody smile of mines as there was still commotion going back and forth from sideline to sideline. I couldn't believe that I did that, but I did. I was proud of myself. I usually don't condone ignorance, but sometimes, you gotta get ignat to let a mofo know that you are serious. After about 30 minutes, we were all called to the middle of the field, where Hoover's coach was waiting.

"Take a damn knee!," he said.

"Looka here boys. What just happened on that field may have been banned in 49 other states that don't know crap about football. But this is ALABAMA! Son, Ramses, what you did was dirty, but *** dammit as I say. If you make a mistake, let it be an aggressive one. If your gonna play dirty, then *** dammit make sure you get filthy. We are gonna run this back again. This time though, I don't want any shenanigans. No fighting, none of that. You can talk more crap out of a bull's ass all day, but we are gonna fine tune each other. Rodney, you ain't been hit like that in a long time son. And quite honestly the last time I seen something hit that hard my wife popped out three boys over a six year span. Take it out on our rivals when the season starts. Now, let's line that Hoover O back up and that multi state defense and play some football. I thought it was a bad idea. Contrary to what I thought, however, the next two hours actually turned out to be a good damn exercise for both teams. They scored five times on our first stringers, but we had two pick sixes. I can't lie, though. Their defense was stout and full of speed. Our O had a hard time moving the ball as we only scored twice. During the last hour as the second teams went at it, I sat over on the bench, relaxing a bit with a few cats from the squad. I was so wrapped up in conversation that I didn't even see Rodney walking over towards us.

"Hey you? Newport?" Everyone just looked at him not knowing what to expect.

"Sup," I said, arising from the bench.

"Good shit out there. Ain't no nigga hit me like that in a long time. Why don't you bring that to Bama with me after next year and we Roll Tide on the whole SEC?"

"I'll think about it man," as I dapped him up.

"You know right now I'm all in on Sparty." He just laughed.

"Just remember yo. The road to any title goes through the SEC. The Slaughter Everybody Conference." I replied back the only way I knew how.

"And you just remember. In the Big Ten, we don't play pretty. 2000. Brady beats Alabama. 2008. Michigan beats Florida, doing what the Sucknuts couldn't do the year before in the national championship. Oh trust, you don't slaughter all." He shook his head up and down as a smirk came across his face. I did the same as he back peddled and took off back towards the Hoover sidelines. Oh yea. I had a homeboy for life in Rodney. What a coincidence it would be if we met for the national title years from now.

"A man, question." It was one of the dudes from Beverly Hills.

"Since we cool, would you get mad if I dropped the N bomb in a good way?" I just looked at him.

"Try it if you want to nigga!," Carlos yelled from the other end of the bench. It was evident from his tone that ol' boy wasn't gonna try it, even though it was wild that Los dropped the N bomb himself in that situation. It was now almost three in the afternoon and we were on the way back home for dinner and a wind down. Tep was in the back knocked out like he had been playing for a few hours, when all he did was chill on the sidelines. I was up front just making random talk with Mr. Turner for the quick trip back.

"You know when you hit ol' boy in the mouth out there; it reminded me of my college days." He flashed a bowl ring in my face.

"Who you play for sir?"

"I took my tail to Texas. Longhorn Country. I wore that burnt orange for four years. I wanted to get out of state for college. All I had known my whole life was Alabama. I wanted to be different. I was a four year starter at Hoover. Defensive End to be exact. My momma used one of my relatives address who stayed up there and drove me to school every day. Man we did the damn thing on the field. When I got my full ride offers, I had some tough decisions. I brought it down to Mississippi State, Ole Miss, Bama, Auburn and Texas. I for damn sure was leaning to roll tide. On the recruiting trip to Texas, I met a brother by the name of K.T. His real name was Kerry Terry. This somma bitch had me at a party that was so live that I told the coach the next day that I was committing.

Yea I got down for the first three years, starting and doing the damn thang. In the first game of my senior year, boom. I tore my Achilles. Right then and there, I told myself that was it. I graduated with a Bachelor's in criminal justice, and here I am on the Birmingham Police force."

"What bowl is that ring from?," I asked.

"This from when we kicked Loser Sooners ass in the Cotton Bowl. The Red River Rivalry. That day, it was more like a Texas gun fest because we were shooting down anything in a red jersey." I was amazed by his story. It was one thing to know he was a detective. It was another to know he had a troubled past and still made it. It was a totally different thing to know he shared in one of my favorite passions in life and played it on a level that only a few of us can achieve. I indeed felt a sense of renewal in my spirit. We got home, showered and all of us enjoyed a bomb meal that Fred's wife had thrown together. It was southern by all means. Collard greens with ham hocks, baked Mac-n-cheese with diced ham topped with bread crumbs, hot water cornbread, slow roasted pork ribs, chitlins with some huge hog maws in 'em, pinto beans, peach cobbler and some red Kool Aid. Man I see why this brother was a little bit on the heavy side. If I had a woman like this cooking for me every night, I'd be a hefty sized brother myself. The itis crept in slowly after that and I saw it was 7:30. Time had flew by quick as ever.

"You wanna go shoot some hoops bruh?"

"Naw Tep, I got the itis bruh. I'm about to head upstairs and call it a night."

"It's aight," he responded.

"You know light skinned taking over and you don't want this L." All I could do was shake my head as he exited the back door rapping some Drake. I was frozen stiff looking up at the ceiling, eyes wandering to God knows where. I thought about the last three days that I was here. I thought about the lessons that I had learned in that time. I saw the side that wasn't too pleasant. I saw where I didn't wanna end up. Today, I saw that I was accepted no matter where I was from, simply because I knew how to play a sport. I thought about that time at USC, when those dudes from Compton basically told me that I wasn't black because I was privileged.

Then I thought about today to where none of that mattered. It was just mess talking based on the state you played football in. It had nothing to do with your upbringing. I saw today that everyone in this world wasn't the same. I saw that there were people who could care less about your personal life. All they cared about was having fun and being competitive. I knew that on our schedule, Saturday and Sunday was open to just relaxing. I, however, didn't want to. I wanted to continue to relish in this experience. I didn't want any days off. At the least, I could ask Mr. or Mrs. Turner what books they had to read so that I could expand my mind even further. If not that, at least I could take a trip to the library. I thought about what greatness I would analyze next. I thought about this until I drifted off into a deep sleep.

3 WADE IN THE WATER

Sometimes life is complete opposite
we are baptized by fire
and burnt by water
ice is the worst pain and heat makes you feel comfortable
so is the Devil good and God evil
Thats for your mind to decide

"There is a severe flood warning for Jefferson County and the state of Alabama as a whole. Torrential downpours and heavy winds will continue on through Monday. Folks are being advised to stay in your homes unless for absolute emergencies."

Watching the news on a Sunday down here was definitely different from anything in Newport Beach. It didn't even have to rain heavy where I was at for people to go crazy. If you even spit on the ground in Southern California, a national emergency was called because let's face it, California people cannot drive in the rain.

"I swear boss it looks like Oregon right now," Tep said as

he peeked out the curtain. It was Sunday night and we had finished off a good day of church service. It was my first time ever going to church in the South. Now, I loved Jesus, don't get me wrong. However, these southern folks took worshiping God to a whole new level. We were literally in church from 11 a.m. to 4 p.m. What made it even worse is that none of the windows were open and they didn't have any A/C. I know it wasn't summer time, but it was still hot in that joint. It was like they were trying to sweat the sin out of your body completely. Also, it was my first time going to one of those huge, over the top, crazy built Baptist churches. I just never got what they meant by First Baptist or Second Baptist. I'd probably be more amazed when I saw a church that was named The Last Baptist church. Then and only then would I know that the end of the world was near. Things were kicking up outside something serious.

"Oh shit man! Ram, yo! Lightning just struck a house across the street! It's on fire!" I shot up off the couch to look out the window and he wasn't lying. I raced over to the phone and called 911. The only problem was that I didn't know what street I was on or the name of the area. Basically, those people were crap outta luck if they were depending on me. I gave the dispatcher the best description that I possibly could. The only thing I got accurate was Southside. Me and Tep continued looking outside as this fire was constantly growing. We did hear sirens after about five minutes, but the sight was still one for sore eyes.

The Taylors' had taken off earlier in the evening before things got bad to go visit some friends in another county or city. I really couldn't remember. When I saw fire, it instantly brought back bad times for me. My parents died in a blaze of glory on the side of the highway. It was something that I still couldn't get over because I wanted to know the truth. We continued to watch as the fire trucks pulled up. The rains didn't do anything to stop the fire. It may have slowed the spread, but the house was half ablaze. If I could estimate, it was at least $800,000 gone down the drain.

"Tep. What do you think when you see fire man?"

"Don't ask me that bruh?" He looked at me kind of weird when he said that. I didn't know if I had said something wrong, but I certainly didn't want to rub him the wrong way.

"Sorry bruh. Whatever bad memory I served up I didn't do it on purpose." All of a sudden he just put his head down.

"Sit on the couch bruh. I got something to confess." He went over first and I just looked at him. I was trying to process what I was about to hear. I slowly made my way over and sat next to him, watching him with his face in his palms on the edge of the couch.

"I was 13 years old bruh. For years I had been picked on and discriminated against all because my mama was a minority. I mean, I went to church, so I thought everything and everybody was supposed to embrace love. One night, I just got fed up with everything that was going on involving her. She was a woman who worked her tail off to give me the best life possible. I hated white people man. And it's crazy cause I'm half white.

One night, I snuck off on my bike. I went riding around a random neighborhood in Tualatin. It was summertime, so the sun hadn't dropped yet. A police car drove by, but they thought I was just a kid enjoying his summer. They waved to me and I waved back. I stopped in a park and just sat there until it got completely dark. Out of my pocket, I pulled out a lighter and a cloth. I was smart enough to have gloves on so that no fingerprints could be found. At about nine o'clock, I made sure everything was clear. I saw a car pull up and the token American family got out. Two white parents and three happy kids. They even had the white picket fence around their house. I gave 'em about twenty minutes. I biked it up real slow to their crib. There was a huge bush on the side of the house, which wasn't uncommon because this was Oregon and we had more green stuff than the Amazon. I lit the cloth, put it on the bush and hauled off into the night. When I got home, I honestly thought that they would see a lil brush fire and put it out. I didn't know that I had just caused a massive tragedy.

Turns out that little fire I started turned into a big ball of flames. As the family was trying to flee once they discovered the fire, the father was carrying out his daughter when he tripped and fell down the stairs. They both broke their necks instantly, dying on the spot. The mother left her other two children outside to go back in for them, not knowing they were dead. When she went back in, the upper floor collapsed and she burned to death in the house. Two kids were left without a sister, a father and a mother, and I was the one to blame. I gotta live with that every night. With every breath I take. You know when we were watching that intro video to Birmingham at the center? I was tore up inside. Every time I seen a white person light a black establishment or anything on fire, a little bit of life left from inside of me. I'm taking this with me to my grave and so are you. You are the only one who knows this bruh. I don't know why, but God somehow knew you would be the one to have an open ear to listen to me and not condemn me to hell. I dunno. I sometimes feel that I already signed my death sentence with the devil." The tears continued to flow from his eyes. You could see the pain on his face and hear it even more through his voice.

"Do you know the song Wade in the Water?," I asked him.

"Yea I heard about it."

"Sing it for me?" He looked at me weird.

"Sing it for me bruh? Like, all BS aside. Sing it for me? After a little hesitation and a nigga why is you asking me this look, he began:

"Wadeeeeeee in the waaaaaaater. Wadeeeeeeeee in the waaaaater. children Waaaadeeeeeeee in the waaaaater God's gonna trouble the waaaaater"

"Now how did that make you feel? Honestly?"

"Man......no different really. What was I supposed to get outta that? I mean.....really?"

"Just listen to the song man. The water. What you think of when you see water? Cleansing. Purity. Rebirth. Maybe you need to take that dip man. It ain't over and God ain't through with you yet man. Look at how my life turned out." Things got real quiet as all Tep did was stare at me.

"Baptism don't save man. Don't believe the hype bruh." I wanted to say something, but I had to hold my tongue. Right now, he was in another mind frame and I needed to let him collect himself before we spoke again.

"Well I'm headed to bed man. Goodnight." I left him down stairs in the living room pondering his thoughts while I went up to relax and getaway. I got to the room and randomly opened a drawer. In it I found a dusty old bible. This thing was so beat up and old that it looked like the original Bible that was written. I blew the dust off that thing and cracked it open. You could tell this was old because of all the pen and ink marks in here. There were notes galore on every page. It kind of amazed me that someone could study this book in such a way. I never in my life read The Bible front to back. I only read snippets. Screw it I said. I closed my eyes and randomly flipped through the pages. Wherever I landed, that is what I would read. I stopped flipping, opened my eyes and there I was in the book of Mark, in chapter 12. And it read:

Mark 12:14-17

1. And when they were come, they say unto him, Master,

we know that thou art true, and carest for no man: for thou regardest not the person of men, but teachest the way of God in truth: Is it lawful to give tribute to Caesar, or not?

1. Shall we give, or shall we not give? But he, knowing their hypocrisy, said unto them, Why tempt ye me? bring me a penny, that I may see it.

1. And they brought it. And he saith unto them, Whose is this image and superscription? And they said unto him, Caesar's.

1. And Jesus answering said unto them, Render to Caesar the things that are Caesar's, and to God the things that are God's. And they marvelled at him.

I honestly didn't get it. I didn't even comprehend what it was saying. However, I figured that it would pay dividends off for me one day in my life so I jotted the scripture down in my phone before closing the book. I had always been spiritual. I just wasn't a religious person. What I mean is this. I delved deep into everything historically, but when it came to God, I was kind of nervous. I was a little bit intimidated. I mean, the way I seen God, it's that He was beyond a mysterious figure. What if God was two people? Three people. He said Lord of Lords. So I wondered is there more than one Lord? He said He is a jealous God and that He would not have any other Gods before him. With that said, I started to wonder was there more than one God in existence? It was so much mystery surrounding The Bible and the stories it entailed that yea, I was a little skeptical to delve deep into it. It would be something that I would have to conquer one day if I truly wanted to master the universe. For now though, I decided to just be the abnormal, yet normal sixteen year old kid from Oklahoma, who was reborn in Newport. As I started to head to bed, red and white lights flashing everywhere, I thought about my mom and dad who met their demise by fire. I closed my eyes and saw a vision.

"Baby, we gotta stop this real soon. That boy is gonna lose us if we keep this up."

"Sugar plum what you talking about? This is what keeps the food on the table. We ain't always doing this. It's once in a blue moon and it's a huge score every time. Just trust me on this." It was like they were oblivious to me as I sat in the back seat when we were rolling down I-10 on the way to Houston. My parents had some James Brown playing in the whip. I don't know where we were or how far we were from the city. I looked outside and saw nothing but darkness and a few lights that were on the freeway. I couldn't speak to save my life. It was just me, there, looking at them. They kept talking for about another 15 minutes when all of a sudden, lights appeared in their rear view mirror. They were creeping up fast until they were damn near on my parents back bumper.

"**WHO IN THE HELL IS THIS?!,**" my pops yelled, as he reached for his semi automatic weapon under the seat. As he was doing that, another car pulled on the passenger side and started to ram them. I couldn't feel anything as I was just there like I said before. Pops sped up and my mama was screaming.

"**Shutup! Shutup! We'll be okay!**" We got rammed again, but this time, pops lost control of the car. He tried to regain control, but it was to no avail. The car flipped over numerous times until it landed in an embankment on the side of the freeway. I was unfazed. My mom, she was clinging on to life, hanging halfway out the window. My pops was still struggling to get free, even though he was covered in blood and had probably broken every major bone in his body. I saw four pairs of legs walk up on the car. One face looked down and stared right at my dad.

"Well waddup Skeelo? You remember how I told you that if you played me for my money, that you and the whole family would suffer?" He looked over in the back seat.

"Well, I don't see that son of yours in here, so consider himself lucky. However, for you, well, you ain't so lucky." Pops couldn't say anything back as he was writhing in pain. Outside my window, I saw liquid falling all down the windows and the smell of gasoline soon over powered my young nostrils. Then, an old familiar tune was soon sung outside of the car.

"Waaaaadeeeee in the waaaaaater. Waaaaaaadeee in the waaaaater children Waaaaaaadeeeeeeeeeee in the waaaaater God's gonna trouble the waaaaaaater"

"Wade in the water Skeelo, Cause you gone damn sure need a lot of it." Four shots rang out. Suddenly, a match was dropped and the screams from my dad were heart wrenching. I was just there. I couldn't feel the fire, nor the heat, but I could smell the burning flesh of my moms and pops.

"Dad," I yelled out. I was finally able to talk. **"Dad! Dad! Dad!"**

"YO RAM!" I shot up in a pool of my own sweat. Tep was there, grabbing my arms. "Bruh, you aight. You were in here screaming and hollin for your pops mane!" I tried to catch my breath, but I couldn't.

"Chill here man. Imma go get you some water." Tep ran downstairs while I collected myself. I didn't know what time it was or what. I didn't even know where I was at. All these years I had wanted the truth and answers as to how things really went down that fateful night. If my belief in God had faltered some, it had been reassured right then and there as I finally had clarity. I can't say they weren't asking for it due to the life they were living. Still, no one deserves to die in that fashion.

"Here man. Drink up."

"Thanks T." I sipped this cold water like it was a cold beer.

"Yo, they finally put that fire out across the street. Look out the window. The rain stopped and everything, but that joint is damaged beyond belief." I slowly got up and walked towards the window where I seen a crowd of people gathered outside huggin' each other and consoling one another. The rain had indeed ceased, but the damage was done. A house was gone, trees were in the middle of the street, car windows were broken and a whole wake of destruction lie in front of us.

"Yo I got a text from the Taylor's bruh. They say their good. Over in the next county. They'll be home tomorrow." That was good to hear, but I was locked in on the vision across the street. The impact that fire had on this small triangle of people was completely random. Then again, I had to remember that nothing random occurs in this world. It is all a part of a bigger plan. Tep burned a house down. My parents burned in a vehicle. These folks across the street house burned to the ground. Then, as I sat here alone. I began to sing to myself.

Wade in the water
Wade in the water
Children wade, in the water
God's gonna trouble the water
Who's that young girl dressed in red
Wade in the water
Must be the children that Moses led
God's gonna trouble the water

Who's that young girl dressed in blue
Wade in the water

Must be the children that's coming through,
God's gonna trouble the water, yeah

You don't believe I've been redeemed,
Wade in the water
Just so the whole lake goes looking for me
God's gonna trouble the water

Wade in the water
Wade in the water
Children wade, in the water
God's gonna trouble the water

"Yo how'd you know that whole song yo?" I turned around to see Tep staring dead at me.

"I dunno man. Truthfully, I never even heard the song past the initial lyrics. For some reason though, it just popped into my head, more or less my soul. What you think it means man. Wade in the Water? I mean, I don't think it was just some random song that black folks created to pass the time by. I mean really big dog. What does it mean?" Tep smiled for a minute.

"Yo, I may be light and damn near white, and not a history buff like yourself, but gone sit down fam. We gone rap on this." I sat down thinkin' to myself, what does this dude know about some black history? Actually, he knew more than I imagined.

"Look here man. Everybody refers this song back to Harriet Tubman leading the slaves to freedom. Something about going through the water so the dogs wouldn't find their scent. That made hold true in some aspects, but you know this song actually goes back to the biblical days right?" I just looked at him crazy.

"Get the hell outta here man. What biblical days?"

"Look here man," as he for once looked like he was about

some business in his life besides the basketball court.

"Wade in the Water was a decoded spiritual joint man. It was revolved around baptism, where you know that in the Christian faith, it was the process of being reborn or giving your life to Christ. Look up John the Baptist and then holla at me." I mean, I really couldn't say anything because he had a valid point. I never thought about that song like that. Actually, I never heard of it coming from The Bible.

"I thought you didn't read The Bible."

"I never said I didn't. You assumed I didn't." That lil goofy grin came across his face.

"Okay Chris Tucker." We shared a laugh, but he had taught me a valuable lesson. Never assume and furthermore, never stereotype. I got upset in my life when my own looked at me as not being black. I looked at my man as not knowing black history. And yes I say black history because the folks in The Bible...well...y'all already know that. Skin of bronze. Hair like sheep's wool. Yep. It sounds like a brother to me. We spent the rest of the night choppin' it up until we both decided to call it a night. As he lay on that couch snoring louder than a freight train, I simply stared at the ceiling. In my head, I was hummin' the song once again. As I was hummin', a huge roar of thunder shot through the night sky. I turned my head to see nothing but rain outside the window. Maybe I needed a baptism of my thoughts. Maybe my baptism was coming. Maybe I had been baptized already and didn't even know it.

4 THE DEFINITION OF BLACK

How does a man survive his toughest challenge
when the battle is against his norm
How does he conform to something he is not accustomed to
when he never accepted it
Why does a man see a bigger picture
even if it causes him to lose his own frame
Why does he still put blame on himself
even when it is not his responsibility
How does he find humility in situations like these
How can one ever question his heart
How can he stay on a path
when even the path he's on can lead him astray
or towards the right place
just at the wrong time
How does a man put himself beneath the next
by his own free will
How does lookin up at the sky and saying yes
ensure his treasure will come at the end
Its hard...I aint gone even lie

The final week of our visit was here. From what I had experienced in the previous week, I knew that I would forever be changed by this experience. The Turners made it back safely Monday morning around 10 in the morning. Trees had collapsed on the freeway where they were so they just stayed in the safety of their friends home until they could get back safe. As we ate breakfast, because he brought me and Tep back nine Egg McMuffin sandwiches, he asked us both a question at the kitchen table.

"If I told you boys that something amazing in this world was 104 years old, would you go with me to see it?"

"Heck yea Mr. Taylor." Tep was so rude talking with his mouth full of food.

"I freaked out the first time, but I ain't freaking out this time. I'm ready for whatever. What about you Ramses?" I looked over at Mr. taylor.

"Sure sir." He shook his head up and down.

"Get ready boys. The most important day of your life is here. After y'all eat, take a break and chill. We leaving at 12, because you gone need some time to think before we bounce." He walked out of the kitchen and left us to ponder on what we were about to see. 104 years old? All I could think about was some major part of history. What building or Civil War cemetery would we be going to? I didn't know and neither did Tep. When 12 rolled around, we jumped in the truck.

Mr. Taylor told us to get some sleep because we would be on the road for a while. Neither one of us paid him any attention. The way he had hyped this up, we wanted to see every part of the road in which we were traveling. I can't lie, the Alabama scenery wasn't one that made your jaws drop. It was simple and flat. It was the real country. One hour passed and we were still on the road. I thought that this dude was really taking us somewhere crazy. I really thought it was an old war cemetery. Tep was good and gone by now as we continued driving. Another hour passed and it was much of the same. Flat land and nothing much to see. Then, after about another 30 minutes of driving, at 2:37 p.m, I saw the sign. MIDWAY, ALABAMA. I didn't know what a Midway, Alabama was and had never heard of it in my life. All I knew is that if there was a picture next to the word country in the dictionary, then this place would be that picture. It was an old, rural farm town from the looks of it. The buildings looked old and something out of the early 1900's. I saw elderly black folks walkin' the streets. It really looked like a serene and chill area. Suddenly, we stopped in front of a white house.

"Get out boys." Tep was up by now and we both stepped out. We watched as Mr. Taylor walked up the steps of this old, white abandoned house. He stood there, just looking at it. We didn't know what it meant to him, nor what he was trying to teach us.

"Come on up here fellas. Lemme explain to you some history." We walked up behind him, but we were skeptical of these steps, so we kept our feet planted on the ground right in front of them.

"This right here. This place...right here. This is where my grandmother Arrilla was from. We called her Bell. Raised right here in this house In this little quaint town in the middle of nowhere. She had nothing more than a third grade education. But boy oh boy. She raised 9 kids here and they all made it into something great. She gone now. Gone and moved on to roasting duck for Jesus as she always used to say. Can you believe that?," as he turned around and looked at us. "Who says that? She always used to say to us as kids learn to cook, because one day I'm gonna be roasting this duck for Jesus. We thought she was nuts back then. She was a church going woman. She believed in no A/C like most of the old folks.

Remember when I took y'all to church that day and y'all swore the devil was sitting on the altar? Well when you came to church in this here little town, you literally felt like the sun lived on top of you. You'd lose 25 pounds from church service and that's without dancing and acting a plum fool for Jesus. She gone now boys. She gone now." Mr. Taylor let his head down, shook it and walked back towards the car.

"C'mon. We almost there." Neither one of us said anything. I especially didn't say nothing. Hell, I didn't even remember seeing my grandparents, let alone know that they existed. It was hard for me to comprehend what I had just saw. I would have given my left arm to enjoy time with my real grandma and grandpa. Don't get me wrong, I appreciate the adoptive grandparents that I had, but I never got that feeling of closeness with them. I never got those down south home cooked meals. I just got meals. I never got a real Christmas with snow and throwing snowballs. All of mines had 80 degree weather and palm trees. On Christmas day, I was riding my bike with my dad along the Pacific Coast. I loved them as I said, but that authentic family experience is something else I tell you man. I yearned to have all of my cousins in one spot, playing games and kicking it. After about another minute down a dusty road, we stopped in front of a blue house, where there was an elderly woman in a rocking chair on the porch. Next to her, a dog. A golden retriever to be exact. As we got out the car, she spoke and spoke clearly.

"Frederick Douglass Taylor." Me and Tep both stopped dead in our tracks. I don't know if we were more amazed at his full name or the fact that this elderly woman spoke so clear.

"How did you know it was me?," he asked as he planted a kiss on her cheek.

"Oh now my hearing has always been good. I know how ya feet drag when you come see me. Who you got with you? I don't recognize those footsteps." This woman was amazing. You could tell she was blind by the cloudy color on her eyes, but to decipher who someone was by how their feet sounded was more than amazing.

"Big mama, this is Ihmotep and Ramses. Two young men who I have had the privilege of mentoring to for the last week."

"Ihmotep and Ramses," she said.

"Like the Kings of our Ancient homeland. Touch my hands young men." As we went to each side of her, we each stuck out one hand and she grasped em.

"You. You on the left. You are a king. Yet you struggle to be who you are. You fear that you aren't accepted by your own kind. We love you. We need you. We need our kings!" I looked at Tep because this woman has just summed my life up with a few words and she didn't know me, nor could see me.

"And you baby. You on my right. Your blood has king running through it. Yet you are scared because those around you for so long have told you that your blood is wrong. Yet you are a king." Tep was dead silent and motionless. He was awestruck much like I was.

"Sit down babies. Let me tell you a story." We sat on the stairs and looked at Mr. Taylor. He nodded his head up and down as if to say I brought you both to the right place. The dog went back by here side.

"104 years ago, I was born to a poor mother and father, down in the delta in lower Mississippi. I had to raise chickens and get our food from the ground. We ate red dirt. We ate berries and slaughtered chickens to eat. But the best food that we all had was the food of The Bible. I know The Bible from front to back and have read it over 900 times. That was before I lost my sight. But with my lost of sight, I gained something extra. My sight. I see now more than ever before.

Back in 1950, I was 40 years old, with three children when we moved over to the town of Midway. It was one of the few places us colored folks could come and live without being harassed by the Klan or police. It was a tight knit community over here. We had colored schools, colored stores. Everything was kept in the community. We were community.

When I hear of the evils in the world today, I think to myself, its because there is no community. There is no love. What happened to Jesus in schools? What happened to kids respecting their parents? What happened to life babies? What happened to life? All of my babies are deceased now, but they lived. They loved. They were honorable, church going and I know they are a part of a praise team in the sanctuary right now. My grandbabies, all 39 of em including greats and great greats, I love em. I pray for em. I cast the blood of Jesus upon their spirits. I cast his love and blood upon you now. Fred, my baby. He is my child, even if I didn't birth him. You two babies, you are now my children. Because in community, we have more than one mother and father. We have what we call a village.

The village raises the children as a collective. If one starves, then none of us eat until we all have food. If one has no shoes, then we don't walk until everyone has shoes. We are community. They say community is dead. Black on black is alive. And they are right. Our babies are killing their own relatives and they don't even know it. They are killing their brother and their sister. We must live for the moment. The worst thing I want to do is get to heaven and hear God say my people are extinct. For if we become extinct, then what started this earth will die. You are kings babies. Remember that. It seems like yesterday when our people were the greatest form of life on this earth. We sat on thrones. We gave the earth life. Do you know what its like to be able to see the melanin in our skin? It is the greatest feeling in the world.

Jesus, Jesus himself babies had the same melanin running through his veins and his skin. They crucified him, which told us that we were to feel the same punishment. In the end, however, we still nourish man who want to see us deceased, because we all need love to survive. You don't let ignorance become of you. Oh come here baby. Come here. You who is the king. The ruler. The one who once feared his own being. Come baby come."

I kind of looked around acting as if I didn't know who she was talking too. I walked over slowly, which wasn't much seeing that I was right there on the steps. I stopped right in front of her.

"Give me your hand." I slowly reached my hand out to her. The minute she grabbed it, it instantly felt like a rush of another spirit came inside of me. I couldn't describe it, but it was like something new was inside of me.

"Baby, you shall fear nothing. You shall lead nations to victory. You shall sit on your throne and lead every man with melanin to the Promised Land. Reach into my pocket baby. There is a piece of paper that will tell you of the great future that you have coming." Slowly, but not out of fear, I reached in her right side robe pocket and grabbed the piece of paper. I opened it up slowly and read it.

Wade in the water

Wade in the water

Children wade, in the water

God's gonna trouble the water

I didn't know what it was about this song, but it was starting to sink into my spirit.

"Sing it to me king. Sing it to me." I sung it too her and she then told me something that I didn't understand.

95

"The water will save you. Remember how Jesus baptized people? The water will save you. Yet your baptism will be dry. I love you son." I seen her crack a smile and take a deep breath. It would be the last breath that she took.

"Fred! Fred! She's not breathing! Help her! Help!" Fred walked up to me and just removed my hand from hers.

"I don't think she needs any help son. Trust me, what she is looking at right now is more peaceful than any country setting. C'mon let's go." I was ballin tears and through my water stained eyes, I saw Tep crying on the steps. I didn't know this woman from the man on the moon, but she left a lasting impression on me as if she were my own mother. I couldn't move, literally. Fred and Tep had to grab me and drag me to the car because I was that emotional. I never had felt like this towards anyone that I had just met. It was indeed to say the least, the most rewarding, yet saddest experience that I had ever encountered in my young sixteen years of life.

We got in the car and headed back towards Birmingham. It was kind of a serene and quiet drive as all hearts and minds were still on what we had just encountered. As I looked into the Alabama countryside, it became more and more evident that my life was in these flatlands. It was untouched and undiscovered. I hadn't even begun to live my life yet, but these two weeks brought more outta me than any other time. About an hour in, Tep was sleep, but I was still wide awake. I was now holding the paper in my hand that I pulled outta Big Mama's robe.

"Wade in the water," I whispered. I suddenly seen how the sky had changed from clear to overcast, showing that we were back to the now minimal rain that was left over from the big storm. As I read the paper over and over, I happened to glance back up and I swore on everything that I love that I saw a face in the window.

"Stop the car Fred!" He slammed on the brakes and

moved over to the side of the freeway.

"What happened?" I got out and just started running across the open terrain.

"Ramses! Where are you going?" I heard him, but I didn't hear him. I kept running until God himself told me to stop. There it was, a trench in the ground full of water. It wasn't ideal for swimming or drinking. The only thing that could last in this water was the horse sized mosquitoes that Alabama produced. I tip toed around the muddy trench being careful not to fall in. I looked back in the distance to see Tep and Fred now outside of the car wondering what the hell I was doing. I looked on the ground for I don't know what. Then, I saw it. Right on the edge of the trench, there was a silver casing about the size of a photo album. I didn't question myself. I just grabbed it and picked it up. I took off running towards the car as if someone were chasing me and trying to kill me.

"I found it! I found it!," I kept yellin' as I got closer. Once I got to them, they were both looking at me like I was crazy.

"What in the world is that?," Tep asked?

"I dunno man. It was like a spirit stopped me and told me to go to the water because something was there." The looks on all three of our faces said it all. We were all shocked beyond belief.

"Let's go home. We'll check it out in comfort," Mr. Taylor said. We got back in the truck and completed the last hour back to Birmingham. After a quick stop to get some grub, we were back in the house and at the living room table. Fred's wife had joined us and even she was scratching her head wondering what this was.

"It looks like a photo album in a silver case," she said.

"There's a lock on it to open, but where is the key?" Right then, as if on command, the lock mechanism just popped. We were all in stunned silence. This wasn't typical black folks.

Y'all know had this been a rated R movie we would've all ran out of the house and never come back, 'cause black folks don't mess around with ghosts.

"Well, who is gonna do the honors?," Tep asked. All three looked over at me as if I were the only choice. I mean, I did have the vision that led me to it, so it would only be right.

"Alright. I got it." I said that nervous as hell as if I were a pig going through the bacon gauntlet. With a deep breath, I opened it up. Inside there were a bunch of papers. We all just stared at this bundle of paper. I mean, did I really run through a field for a case with nothing but paper?

"Take the top sheet off. See what's underneath." I looked at Tep when he asked me that. I was nervous to see what was underneath. I took off the top sheet. What lay before our eyes was indeed more than history, but we still didn't know the meaning of what we had. It looked like a book that was written back in the days when black folks were out and about on the plantation.

"Right Book, Wrong Chapter," Fred's wife said.

"Seems like an ironic title. Open it up." I reached in for it, but was very careful due to the condition and age of this thing of how I handled it. I didn't want it to rip up on contact and then none of us would never know what was inside. We took it out very carefully. After blowing off about five pounds of dust, we actually saw that it wasn't in as bad of shape as we had all thought before. The casing that it was in saw that it held up well over the years.

"1939 it says it was written," Tep holla'd.

"That's the year my grand mammy was born. On a lowly April 28th day. Open it up man." Why was I so nervous to open up a book? I mean, it was just a book. What harm or foul had a book ever caused to the normal man? Then, I thought about something in that moment. I thought about The Bible. How throughout all of its books, men have waged heated debates on what is real and what is not. They argue and sometimes damn near come to blows. It even altered the course of history. The white slave masters used The Bible to control the black slaves in America. Some radical groups used it to justify their hate and bigotry towards others. The Bible wasn't simply a book. It was something much more deeper than that. I opened up to the first page and sunk in the words. *"To those who will read, know this was written with the blood of those enslaved by their own and sold off to even more despair"* We figured that told us all what we needed to know.

"Flip to a random page man." I shooed off Tep as the rest were steady looking over my shoulder. As I slowly flipped to what would be page 234, I began to read the passage that would change my life forever.

....And then they had what they called the house negro. He manipulated master by manipulating him that his skin was not of melanin pigmentation. He was simply a mistake in the eyes of God. He catered to and enhanced the white man's knowledge on what he owned. Displaying their weaknesses. He saw early that if you took the head of the house and cut it off, that the children would be like the roach with no antenna. It would have no direction. It would have no figure and would emulate the woman. Hoping that in turn that he would one day become like woman so he would not reproduce. And the world would be full of men who were lovers of men, and no more reproduction would occur. We would become extinct. That was not all, as the house negro in another sense urged master to impregnate the black female.

The genes would become strong to make yet another man. Kill every 1st daughter and let only the second remain. Then it would be just enough women to procreate for his profitable gain. And once their use was over, they would be taken to the field and slaughtered. Buried where no one would ever find their bones. For the DNA which is life was in them, and he wanted them ever so nonexistent. When the babies grew old they would fight. They wouldn't see their lineage. They would see he's dark and he's light. They would see that he's brown and he's not as brown. They would hate each other due to light and dark, not realizing that it was a part of the plan to keep them apart.

The house negro would sleep on the good sheets provided in the home. On a good bed and rest comfortably. He was hated, but his smarts were too much for the master not to use him. However, he was not smart enough to see that he was being used. He urged master to bring forth entertainment of slave babies. Making them fight to the death. And the slave, with no knowledge and lack of education saw this as great. Wanting to be the top slave to possibly earn his rite of passage into the home permanently.

The house negro made this all happen. And his mission was accomplished until he died. Then the house negro would be buried in the same manner as the slaves. He was then useless. All his life he thought he was with no pigmentation of melanin. He however ended up like the rest of the lineage. Dead and gone. So I say now, until all lineages that will expand from this moment. Take heed to the words. If it is not stopped now, the future lineage will be nonexistent. Your sons will emulate the woman and want to become as a woman. You sons will fight each other for supremacy, not knowing it was a part of white supremacy. Your families will wage war over who is darker than who. It has been embedded in the DNA. The chain links must be broken.

When reading some words of that high caliber, you had no choice but to sit back and think. What was said in these writings were exactly what was occurring today. Men had become lovers of themselves. They turned themselves into women through their dress and operations. They began to hate actual women and not want to reproduce. And now, this is applauded, not knowing it is a part of the plot to destroy us. You have brothers fighting over who is lighter and who is darker. I looked at Tep in an instant and thought about how I once viewed him secretly as almost not one of us. I kicked myself in the ass. His Egyptian blood is black blood. Additionally, how in the good hell could I even question someone's blackness when my own blackness was in question to everyone else who had encountered me? I was appalled at myself more than anything. I then realized the title of the book and its meaning. Right Book, Wrong Chapter. The Right Book symbolized who we were. BLACK. We were all black no matter the circumstances. Where we came from, who our mothers was, all of that. The Right Chapter was a little bit more complicated to explain. When you see a book, or better yet read one, people usually have a favorite chapter. You go to anyone about a book let's say with 15 chapters, but one person, or rather everybody says "Just wait 'til you get to Chapter 12. It really gets good."

That's how life is. We look to one chapter being the best, yet fail to see that every chapter which makes up a book plays it own unique part in making that book great. The wrong chapter tells us that there is actually no wrong chapter, but it also tells us that we're screwed up in our ways of thinking that there actually is one. The second meaning behind wrong chapter refers to race. I got bashed for being privileged which again, I couldn't control. Some had seen me as the wrong type of black. I was the black kid that wasn't supposed to exist. I should've been in the projects. I should've been in a single parent home. I should've been in a home with both parents, yet we weren't connected as a family. That is the stereotype amongst us all. My wrong chapter was being privileged, but I had the same book of every black person in America. It was simple. Our book was black, but our stories were different. Yet our lack of thinking makes us think sometimes that this person over here is not true because of how they were raised. Or this person thinks this brother ain't true because of what he doesn't give his life too. Those are the wrong chapters that we read amongst each other, not failing to see that we are all writing and existing in the same book, which is the world.

"This is crazy," Mr. Taylor said.

"She told you the water would save your life. This here. Young brother this book right here. This changes everything you ever knew. I don't even wanna see anymore. It was for you and you," as he pointed to Tep.

"Learn the lesson that you were both ordained to learn from it, because she obviously knew. C'mon honey." Fred and his wife walked away and upstairs to their bedroom. Me and Tep sat at the table still in awe from what we had just read.

"Lemme ask you something Ramses. You remember in the movie The Mummy how Ihmotep was a great priest? You think that's why my parents named me that? You think I am to be a great priest?" I looked at him but I really didn't know how to answer the question.

"Do you think my name being Ramses signifies me literally sitting on a throne like he did? Or do you think that I'm supposed to be the one to start the greatest generation that ever existed? I mean, it was like more than ten Ramses' in Ancient Egypt. Maybe my Egypt is all of Earth and I am the beginning."

We didn't know what to think. That's how powerful this book was. We sat there literally questioning each other well into the evening time. Today was literally about baptism. The water saved me like she said. In the process, it saved all of us. More importantly, I learned that baptism doesn't always involve having your head dunked in a body of water. It sometimes involves just learning something new that enhances your minds and causes you to think differently. Today, I was indeed baptized in a river of wisdom. As Tep left for bed, I sat at the table, humming away.

Wade in the water...

Wade in the water Children...
wade, in the water...
God's gonna trouble the water...
Rest in Peace Big Mama. Rather I say, rest in eternity as the river that baptized me.

5 THE FINAL 48

It was now Wednesday. We were due to leave back Friday morning on our respective flights back to our homelands. Over the last two weeks, me and Tep learned what it I was like on the other side something serious. I met myself and found out that I didn't even know myself. It was 10:48 Wednesday morning and we just came back from breakfast with Mr. Taylor.

"Aight ya'll. You seen the first 48. Today and tomorrow, y'all gone see the last 48. Thank me later." I ain't know what he was talking about, but if it was anything like the first two days I was here, then I was ready. I had seen it all, I believed and nothing could break me now.

"5:00 tonight, we ride out. Rest up." He walked out the kitchen, and me and Tep just laughed away.

"Man dude think we gonna fall for the okey doke again man," he said.

"Whatchu talkin' bout bruh?" You got scared and got driven back to the house."

"You right, 'cause I wasn't ready for that shit. Now that I

know that all of this is meant to break us, what do I have to fear? Let's go shoot some hoops." We got outside and played a few games of horse. We were both headed back to our hometowns soon so we had to get all the bonding in that we could. It was cool that I got to meet someone from a different part of the states who lived in a whole different world than me. We underestimate the value of the meet and greet nowadays with the rise of social media. We would rather meet somebody with a click instead of a handshake. This taught me the value of human interaction. As I thought about this, I looked at my cell phone immediately after we finished up our games. 12:31. We had major time to blow. Instead of jumpin' in the shower real fast, I went back to the room and pulled out my laptop. I always had a knack for writing poetry, so I thought this was a good opportunity to get back into it. I looked at my cell phone again and immediately went back on how we as humans put this over each other. I began to write and I called the piece technology

TECHNOLOGY

I remember once when we were human....riding bikes up and down streets, playing hide go seek, memorizing addresses without dot com added to the end of them, you see I remember when we were human, when 69 wasn't a sex position but a way to call somebody back, when VHS and tape decks had to be rewound, when you actually delivered a girl a message without sending it to her inbox first you see.....I remember when we were human, but what we are now is technologically sound with microchips for brains, and fingertips serving as cars traveling long distances over keyboards, these are the new versions of family trips as Skype has taken the place of walking two blocks to grandma's house, because somewhere along the line, we became bored with one on one interaction and became comfortable when AOL told us that we had mail, and eventually we combined five instruments into one to become..........our cell phones, because our life is now our cell phone, we will die for our cell phones, we can't breathe without our cell phones, we just can't exist without our cell phones, men when we can't find our phones we scramble like quarterbacks cause if our woman finds that and calls a few of those numbers back, all hell gone break loose, women, y'all don't feel beautiful on the inside anymore, so you take 1000 selfies, post 'em to your social feed and hope these lil boys on the outside hit like, all this from my cell phone, something in the shape of a small box that has reminded me of the box that technology has encased us in, you see I used to send my complaints to governors with a pen, but now I hit send with ratchet fights and sex tapes sent to worldstar and youtube, all this from my cellular, I even have the choice of different carriers, the same way humans choose to carry different diseases, because we have become so close to our phones that if they catch a virus we become sick as well, I wouldn't be surprised if the abnormal chips in my phone caused me to get sickle cell, that's why I don't download the ESPN app cause the minute I download that, I may catch HIV like Magic or turn into a woman like Bruce, all this from my cell phone, and the funny thing about these phones is that they told us more about us as time evolved, see we had brick phones when we had hardened minds, we had flip phones when we had flip flop mindsets, but now we have iphones because we are no longer concerned about we, we are only concerned about I, so we'd rather send that hateful text when we have that free connect to wi-fi, and I hate wi-fi, so I'll drop the W and the last I and just go back to if, what IF we never had these cell phones, what IF we never lost the value of human interaction, what IF humans didn't become computers and computers didn't become more human than people, because 20 years ago, I knew all of my contacts, now if I lose my phone, I know no one's numbers by heart, so that's shows you that our heart now beats with a barcode, battery and a serial number, I'm just waiting for the surgery where they put a charger slot in my spine so they can charge me up when I am low on life, *cause now a cell phone has taken over all of our lives, so just imagine the destruction that will occur...................when we all go out of service.*

I showered up and got in a good nap till about 4:30.

"Where y'all at?!," I heard Fred yell from downstairs. I came out the room still a lil bit groggy. Tep was downstairs stuffing his face in the kitchen. I walked downstairs and I saw Mr. Taylor in all black everything.

"It's almost five. Y'all ready to ride?" Tep started laughing.

"What you got for us now? A bank robbery?" Even I had to laugh at that one. With a lil smirk on his face, Mr. Taylor responded with a simple "Maybe." The look on his face looked like he had something planned, but like I said earlier, we were ready. Five came around and we peeled out. Neither one of us asked any questions. It was still daylight outside so nothing to dramatic could be going down. We stopped at a warehouse that was about twenty minutes from his crib. It was old and kinda beat up, but we ain't think nothing of it.

"Let's go," he said. We got out of the car, whispering to each other as we walked behind him.

"This dude think he scaring us," I whispered to Tep. We both got in a good chuckle.

"HURRY UP!!! STOP BULLSHITTIN!!!" Now he was really into his role and we did a slow jog to catch up to him. As we hit the door of the warehouse, he gave three knocks.

"When we get in here, y'all don't say a word. You do what you're told and that's that." The door slid open and we literally were all pulled inside. I saw two big ass dudes who looked like they just ate about 40 humans back to back. All I could think was that this was another test, so nothing would happen to us. As we walked down this long hallway, we finally hit the main part of the warehouse, where I could see the light shining on a man who was tied to a chair. He looked like he had went through the ringer of a few dozen fists as he was bloody and battered.

"Welcome gents! We meet again." I turned to the left to see Gold Mouth and his crew coming out of the darkness. It was about a good 15 of 'em. All of 'em had high power assault rifles.

"Sup famo," as he dapped Fred up. "Welcome back to y'all too. So you see, what we have here is a misunderstanding. Ramses," as he pulled me by the shoulder.

"You see this nigga here. Sitting in the middle of the room. He thought he could play us. Remember the body I showed you last week? Yep, he was responsible. Now, that was my family and I hate it, just hate it, when people mess with my family. So. Now that you family. I want to welcome you properly. Lo, gimme Tina." In my hand, he handed me a custom AK 47 that I had seen the first time we met.

"Ram, I want you to unload on this nigga until you can't hold your arm anymore." I laughed when he said that, simply because I thought nothing would happen. They all laughed with me.

"That's what I'm talking about," Gold Mouth said.

"You already are showing no remorse. Now, shoot this nigga. Stank him." I imagined the scene in Training Day where the white cop yelled **BOOM** and so did the guy. The Denzel took the shotgun and popped him. I ain't think this gun was loaded. I was about thirty feet away from ol' boy and everyone had backed back off to the sides.

"Make me proud youngin."

"Can I count down?," I asked him.

"As a matter of fact, you can. It's this niggas birthday. Let's light candles. On three, make her sing. One.....two." I pressed the trigger and only Jesus knows how many shots came out. I stopped dead in my tracks. This gun was really loaded and I really just shot this dude.

"FINISH THE FUCKING JOB!!!," Gold Mouth yelled. I was too busy breathing heavy and trying to comprehend what I had did. I looked back at Fred and Tep. Fred had a stone cold look on his face at ol' boy in the chair while Tep was shocked beyond belief, lookin' like he was about to piss his pants.

"Give it here," Gold mouth said. "I can't blame you. You only sixteen. This shit don't happen in Newport. But let me show you what it means to finish." He took aim and unloaded the whole banana on this dude. Whatever he did, he really was paying for it. As the shots stopped and the smoke cleared, I seen the most horrific sight of my life. It was at least 100 holes in this guy.

"Now," as Gold Mouth turned back to me. "This is simply round one. Tonight, you and ol' Blake Griffin over there, y'all gone get blood on y'all hands. Don't worry. Cuz gone make sure nothing gets traced back to y'all. We gotta house to raid tonight. Niggas got our stash. More importantly, they got my money and I don't like it when people have my money. So, tonight, y'all gone be trigga happy for me. Consider this your final learning experience out here. Do this, don't bitch up and you leave here with 10 G's each. That might not be shit to y'all as a whole, but give my black ass at sixteen ten stacks and its whatever. Are there any questions?" It was not a game and I didn't answer him because I was honestly scared shitless.

"Ok, no questions. Then, we good. Niko, Yoda, grind his bones up." He turned back to me. "Ya mans looks a lil nervous. Come with me so I can show you how we get rid of evidence." I was pushed in my back and literally forced to walk by one of those oversized hulk type brothers. Fred was off to my right side while Tep was now as pale as a ghost. Two of the other brothers were carrying ol' boys body in front of us. We stopped at this huge machine after about a 70 yard walk. One of them went over to press a button. The noise was hella loud as you can tell it was blades choppin.

"YOU GENTLEMEN SEEN THE MOVIE SAW RIGHT?! WELL IN PART THREE, THE PIGS GOT PUT THROUGH A GIANT MEAT SLICER TO BURY THE JUDGE IN THEIR SLOP! WATCH WHAT THIS MACHINE DOES NEWPORT?!" They placed this brothers body on a conveyor and I watched it slowly go up and up and up until it reached the top. As it dropped in, the sound of bones crushing and flesh slicing up damn near made me puke. All of his blood and guts came out of a side piece and into a giant barrel. The big man went over and pressed the button to off. Gold Mouth looked at me with that evil grin and started to laugh.

"That's a helluva show huh? I like you Newport. You got some nigga in you. Ten o'clock we ride. Load the fuck up and let's bounce."

"Let's go," Fred said as we all walked back towards the entrance. About 50 yards before the door, we broke off to the right to a blue lit room that was full of every gun imaginable. Just imagine the movie Money Talks with Chris Tucker. The scene where Aaron walked him into his room full of guns. Yea, it was exactly like that.

"Grab, load up and go. We meet tonight at the palace. Fred. Famo? Give Blake the Nina Ross. He need something simple. Give my nigga pharoah over there Martha Gibbs."

"What he mean by that Fred?," I asked him. Fred just stared at me as he reached for the wall.

"He talking about the sweeper. The street sweeper. Mrs. 227. She yo' bitch tonight." He handed her to me and I found myself in a world of confusion. This ain't what it was like to be black. It was, however, another element of the world that we lived in.

"Let's go," Fred whispered as he simply took two briefcases with him. We got back to the car. It was dark out and no one was around here for miles.

"This stays closed. If any word gets out, I'll have y'all locked up for life with the booty warrior. Oh he'll put all kind of Crimson Tide in y'all ass. Understand?"

"Yea," I told him. He looked back at Tep.

"Understand me light bright?" He shook his head up and down, sweating as if he was cooking in a rotisserie oven. We peeled back out towards the house. It was a little bit past eight. It was a quiet ride back. We got to the driveway and Fred gave one last word of instruction.

"Go in here. Look under the bed and look under the couch. Y'all war clothes is underneath. Eat up something. We're bouncing out at 9:30. Don't piss me off." He got out the car and slammed the door. I sat in there with Tep as he began to cry.

"What you crying for man?!"

"Man I ain't sign up for this shit man. Man this ain't me."

"I know it aint bruh, but look, if we don't stick this out together, then we don't see home. Let's suck it up and just do what we gotta do. Now let's roll." Tep, shaking his head up and down as he was good for agreed and got out. We made it upstairs to our room, shut the door and looked underneath the couch pillows and the mattress. Black pants, black long sleeved tee and a ski mask. Yea, shit was about to get real.

"Man really. What in the hell is this dude trying prove?"

"I dunno. But he wants a savage. I'll give him a savage." I was already throwin' on my pants, while Tep was still trying to figure out what was exactly going on.

"Man put yo shit on." He really wasn't himself. I could tell he didn't wanna do this. But at this point, it really wasn't any other choice. I learned in life, especially being a black kid in Newport Beach. Sometimes, you gotta do what you don't wanna do, to get where you wanna be. I didn't wanna be there not because of the life, but because I never felt I fit in there. However, I had to do what I had to do to make it. Football and dreams of playing for Michigan State became my motivation. Now, my motivation was getting home in one piece.

"Remember how you blew that house up when you were younger?" His whole demeanor changed.

"Man don't remind me of that."

"It ain't to bring back bad memories. It's to show you that you did something you really didn't wanna do to get even. You don't feel like that now, but back then you did. Now look me in my eyes and tell me do you think I'm rolling with you to die?" He just stared at me. "I need my brother from another. Let's do this." I extended my hand out. He hesitated. After about 20 seconds, he dapped me up.

"One and Done. We go home. Thanks for being my brother." We got up and hugged. It was time for two brothers to do what brothers do. That was stick together and make things happen. The goal was the same. Get home safe. Operation Go Ham was about to go down.

There was a knock on our door at 9:15. I opened it up.

"So y'all look ready, but let me ask you. Are y'all ready?" I held up my shit.

"Do I look like I'm ready?" Tep came behind me.

"Nina Ross is beautiful."

"Whoa, what happened to you Blake? Few hours ago you were damn near in tears."

"Well sir, I learned, sometimes, you just gotta do what you gotta do. I firebombed a house at thirteen for all the hate people shot at my mother. It's a repeat to me." If that was an act, he should have gotten the Oscar. Whether or not it was, he was ready. Fred smiled.

"My youngstas. Let's roll." We got out to the car. I know questions shouldn't be asked, but I was a nosey kid.

"Mr. Taylor?" That's when he cut me off.

"Its Fred right now. And right now, we after corrupt cops. That's who we shot up in that warehouse. My cousin, yea, he on the other side of the law. I let some things slide as long as he keeps it confined to only certain areas. However, you got cops on a payroll who overstep their boundaries and forget that not all of us are good ol' boys. We're meeting up at the palace. It's an area where we make stars outta people. Trust me, the plan is laid out. We got more weaponry than Iraq and Afghan soldiers. Shit we the new Talban in this muthafucka. His name, "Powder." He moved out from Cali years ago and joined the force. He had a side hustle, but he got greedy. Now, he robbed and sabotaged the wrong family. A brother gotta do what a brother gotta do. Now, no more questions. We hit and disappear tonight."

He turned around and started the car up. We were out to dipset through these streets. The ride to the palace wasn't long, as I seen it was an open field where a million trucks it seemed were parked at. As we got out, I saw a combination of gangstas and cops. Gold Mouth in his usual fashion was dead in the middle.

"Welcome all. You know why we're here tonight. Operation Kush. We got police who gone interfere with the scanners. We got a twenty minute window to hit four targets before anyone knows what hits them. Lets pay this off. They want war with ours?! They got it." Nothing else was said as we all jumped back in the vehicles and headed out. I saw that Fred was following one group of three trucks.

"Put ya ski masks on boys. Tep, you got the first shot." The police lights kicked on with the first car and we started hauling ass towards downtown.

"When my brother from the truck enters the joint, that bald head cocksucker at the door gone come up and start talking to me. Get out as soon as we stop. Wait on the passenger side. When he comes up to the window to talk, pop his punk ass at point blank." Just like planned, we pulled up to a lit up restaurant. A swarm of cops entered to the shock of many civilians in there. Fred stayed in as the bald headed white dude came up. Tep had crept out already, ready to go.

"Fred what's going on? We got a warrant boss about some drug activity filtering out of this joint. Hit your scanner for back up." He turned around to talk on his brick. *'POP!POP! POP!'* Tep put three straight in his temple and got back in. He hurried back in and we peeled out.

"Man damn what the hell!"

"What man?," I asked him.

"Man that was easier than I thought."

"Round two is you Ramses! We got five minutes till we hit our next target. They call him Rich. A big ass fuel canister been placed in between his home and his neighbors. Just hit it once and he'll be a hot boy for real. He killed my famo and got the money that belongs to my folks. God bless him and their neighbors." We got to a dim lit block and slowed dramatically. I had one shot and one shot only.

"Two houses away. Get ready." I was already aimed. Just then, he sped up. **"FIRE!!!"** I did. With the first couple of shots, the loudest explosion I had ever heard or seen was upon us. Fred peeled out, but our back window shattered violently from the explosion.

"WOOOOOOOOOOOOOO!!!," Fred yelled out.

"Checkmate." I don't know who I just killed. All I know is that I caused major destruction. God forgive me, because I didn't know what I had just done. As we headed back to wherever, in my head, I saw Big mama. I heard her words. I heard everything she had told me. And in this moment, I realized that I was in the wrong chapter. I was in the wrong book. This story wasn't supposed to happen. Not the story of our people. The initial rush was something else, but the aftermath was something that I wasn't ready for. We got back to the palace about 30 minutes later. We waited until every vehicle, which totaled 13 pulled up. Everyone got out, including seven brothers with some huge duffle bags.

"Drop em!," Gold Mouth ordered.

"In here gentlemen, is over seven million dollars in cold hard cash. To the youngins, Blake, Newport, taste this 50 G's." He threw us both something that we never seen in our lives. To the rest of the crew. Two million split 24 ways. The other five goes into the account. Good job gentlemen." I wasn't a rocket science or a major mathematician, but 2 milli split 24 ways was $83,333 a piece. We took our bread and each went about our business.

When we got back to the house that night, I couldn't sleep. What I had just done was beyond terrible. How could I call myself this amazing black man when I just killed for what divides us in the first place? I don't know who all suffered individually, but I was feeling it the most. I looked over at Tep who was knocked out and oblivious to what had occurred. He didn't have a care in the world seeing that this wasn't his first rodeo on taking somebody out. The fact that the guy he shot was white probably did more justice for him and calmed his soul. Me, I never thought I had a bone of murder in my body. How could it be so easy to grab a gun? That's when I heard the knock at my door. It creaked open.

"You sleep?" It was Fred.

"Nah, not really."

"Come downstairs. It's bout time you knew the truth." I didn't know what he meant by that but I followed." I sat down at the kitchen table.

"You want some orange juice? Coffee? Shot of Hennessey?"

"Like you serious about that shot of Hennessey? I aint never drank alcohol a day in my life." He laughed and went to the cabinet, grabbing a shot glass and the bottle. He sat down and poured it.

"Straight back, tilt ya head and just gulp. Don't try and sip." Screw it I thought. I did exactly what he said. I started to cough more than I ever had in my life. I grabbed my throat and fell to the floor.

"You a rookie I see." I eventually made it back to the table where he was taking a shot himself. As I got myself back together, he threw me an old newspaper that was wrapped in a rope.

"Read the first page." I untied the rope and laid it on the table.

"Corpse found burned to death after horrific accident." It was dated twelve years ago to 2002.

"Yo Mr. Taylor. These my parents."

"Yep, and the men we took out tonight, those were some of them from the organization that killed 'em. Yo daddy never drove to Texas. He always drove through Texas. He drove here. Right here. To Birmingham, Alabama." I was stunned beyond belief. You could hear a rat piss on cotton. That's how quiet I was.

"I remember when he brought you down here when you were two. He asked me then. Would you be the Godfather of my child? I was honored. Matter fact, I have never had anyone ask me to be a Godfather. See my wife can't have kids and I don't wanna adopt. My name will die when I die. But I always told him, that if you ever are not here, he will become my son. It took me twelve years years to find you. The same number it took for me to finally avenge his death.

See Brian. Everything ain't random or by circumstance. Some stuff is ordained or planned and you will never know it unless someone tells you. I brought you here. I told them that I want you in my house. All that shit bout the other side of the trap, that wasn't to scare you. That was to show you exactly what your dad did day in and day out to try and put food on the table. He was legit at the same time, but the game was still callin. That's yo fam that was there. Yo daddy's people. Gold Mouth yo' cousin. He just didn't say it. All them niggas Gold Mouth was with, they yo' family. Sure, we all may do some things under the table to put food on the table, but when you know no other way, that's what happens sometimes." He poured up another shot of Henn Dog and took it back. I guess that one was refreshing because he poured another shot glass full and did the same with that one.

"What do I do from here?"

"You, you go back and let this experience mold you. You don't forget. You will never forget. But you do let it mold you into something better. You've seen both sides of the world we live in now. All you got left is the last 24 hours."

"What's that?," I asked. He poured one last shot and chugged it down.

"Tomorrow, I take you to meet them for the first time since you were four. When you were still Brian Carter and not Ramses Martin. Goodnight son." He got up and walked away, not even looking back. I sat there trying to process everything that I had just been told. It wasn't the easiest thing to deal with at the moment, but I was certainly glad that I finally had gotten to know the truth. They say that the truth sets you free. I indeed knew why the caged bird sings. It was cause it finally got to spread its wings and fly in freedom. That's how my spirit felt after that conversation.

I poured me a glass of OJ and just sat back thinking. *Did Big Mama really think I did a terrible thing?* She said wade in the water and it would save me. It also said in that book: And then they had what they called the house negro. He manipulated master by manipulating him that his skin was not of melanin pigmentation. He was simply a mistake in the eyes of God. He catered to and enhanced the white man's knowledge on what he owned. Displaying their weaknesses.

He saw early that if you took the head of the house and cut it off, that the children would be like the roach with no antenna. The last line was what stayed with me. He saw early that if you took the head of the house and cut it off, that the children would be like the roach with no antenna. I was that roach with no antenna for the longest. I had no sense of direction. After being here for almost two weeks, my clear cut path in life was clear. I just had to obtain it now.

Tomorrow morning came around. I mean, the early part of tomorrow morning. I arose at four o'clock on the dot. I didn't have any crazy dreams that woke me up. It was simply a matter of me just arising. I was beyond tired and groggy. Yet something in my spirit was telling me to get up and do something out of the norm. As quietly as I could, I went to my luggage and pulled out a sweat suit. It was my high school sweat suit. I threw it on with the quickness. I tiptoed it out of the room and down the stairs. As quietly as I could, I disabled the alarm panel and headed out the door. Once I hit the driveway, I took a moment to just clamor at the stars in the night sky. Looking at the stars in the country was much different than looking at them in the city. It seemed like they were more pure out here. I didn't know where I was going, but I started right there in that spot with a simple prayer.

Lord, take me to the place you have designed for me. AMEN.

I took off and began running. Something was telling me to make my way towards downtown. I didn't know how to get there, but in my head, I had a vision of which direction to take at every corner and block. I left my hood off of my head, hoping that any police or neighborhood watch captains wouldn't see me, try to attack me, get their ass beat and then shoot me, only for me to get charged with assault when I am dead. Deep down, I was wishing someone would because after what I went through these past two weeks, especially last night, I was ready for confrontation.

I continued on until I got through the gates of the housing community. I stopped at jogged in place on the corner. A squad car was slowly driving by. The two officers in the car looked at me and spotted the flashlight on me. I threw up my hand for a quick wave and they waved back. They kept going and I did the same. I had a feeling they were watching me from a distance, but still, nothing was going to derail me from my mission right here, right now. That's another lesson that I had learned in my short life. You only wanna deal with right here, right now people. Hangin with the IF crowd will have you being an unsuccessful story. They'll say IF I would've done this. IF that was me in that position. IF I had this girl or man.

True, we all have if moments, but you have people who live off the term because they have nothing else going for them in life. The biggest failures are the IF people. Be the right here, right now person. Right here, right now, this was my destiny. After an hour of running, I still wasn't at my destination. The sun was still down but I knew that it would be arising soon on this spring time day. It was chilly outside, but all this sweat and running had warmed me up. I probably was gonna catch the flu or pneumonia, but I could care less right now. I felt like Allen Iverson at this moment. I thought about the commercial he had while playing for Philly. He woke up at 5:30 in the morning and ran all over the city until he triumphed at the top of the steps where Rocky Balboa ran to as well.

All I could think about is where in the world is my statue of Rocky? Where is my finish line? I kept going and going. Finally after what seemed like forever, I was halfway through downtown. I must have lost at least ten pounds of just pure sweat already. The sun was now starting to creep up over the horizon as I seen the sky starting to get lighter and lighter. At about two hours and some change, I finally made it. Here I was. OAK HILL CEMETERY. I sat in front of it, breathing and curled over at my knees. I was dead tired. I needed water and food badly. I was hoping that for this moment that Jesus could fill me up with his blood and rejuvenate me. After a good ten minute break, I simply walked. I walked the cemetery. Had this been an ordinary day, you wouldn't catch me here. I had a thing for the paranormal, but I deliberately didn't mess with the dead. Spirits get attached to you and you find yourself hanging in the middle of your house.

I didn't know what I was looking for. I walked all the way 'til the end and back. I saw nothing but the same sights. Headstones and the one groundskeeper who was already here. When I got back towards the middle of the cemetery, I just stopped and looked around. The sun was out full and bright now, and it was well past 7 o'clock. I spun around 360 degrees, confused. As I got back to looking towards the front, I saw what I thought was a black figure in the distance. I whipped my head around, but nothing was there. It would've been easy to run, but I God honestly believe that was my sign to walk over in that direction. I began to walk a slow, yet methodical walk. I had no more energy left. After about six minutes, I made my way towards two lonely headstones. There was nothing impressive about them. They were even with the ground. As I stood over them, I thought who could this be but my parents. Fred was supposed to take me to see them, but now, I had met them. I rubbed the grass off of one of the headstones.

"RAMSES MARTIN." I jumped back. I was scared beyond belief. I rubbed my eyes to make sure that what I was seeing wasn't some practical joke. My breathing almost stopped. I finally got myself together and bent over to rub the grass off of the second grave marker. It was unmarked.

"No!," I yelled.

"This cant be happening to me. How the hell am I dead?!"

"RAMSES!!!," wake up. "We're here. Boy you must've been dreaming something vicious the whole car ride cause you was shaking in that seat something serious."

"Wh...what? I wasn't dreaming. I just ran here."

"Naw man. I woke you up. You threw on that sweatsuit with that trash truck juice breath and hopped in the car. C'mon man. Go talk to your daddy." Damn, I had never had a more meaningful dream in my life. I thought about one thing. I saw my headstone. So what inside of me, or what part of me died? That's the million dollar question that I had to figure out. It was eating at me and I knew for a while that I wouldn't be the same for the longest. I got out the car, still feeling the chill of this springtime morning breeze. And boy was I tired. Fred was already light years ahead of me.

"C'mon boy! You ain't that tired!" I literally dragged myself across the burial grounds. I was damn near sleepwalking. When I saw him stop up ahead, I said to myself good. When I got to the headstone, which ironically was the same place in my dream, my heart literally stopped. Fred looked at me.

"You wanna do the honors?" Just like in the dream, the headstone was covered with grass. I bent down to wipe it off. Brian Carter Jr. it read. I stood up and just looked at it for God knows how long. Truthfully, what could I say to a man I didn't know? In my eyes, he was my father, but he wasn't. He wasn't around long enough to make an impact on my life.

"Where's my mom?" I turned around to Fred and he just shook his head.

"Her body. Her body son was long gone when the police got there. Where she lies stills remains a mystery to us all. I looked back to my father's headstone.

"Take me home. I don't wanna see no more." I turned around and walked away.

"Ramses! Rames!" Fred kept callin' me, but I kept walking.

I didn't wanna hear anymore of his stories.

"Sparty said yes!" I stopped dead in my tracks and turned around. In his hand, Fred was holding up a manila envelope.

"You wanna see why I brought you here or are you just gonna keep walkin?!" I ran back to Fred like a wolf was chasing me, even though I was only about 30 feet away. I snatched the folder out of his hands and immediately ripped it open. In it were three letters. Alabama, Sparty and Florida State all came callin'. They all said the same thing. They were inviting me to the campus for a tour. Three top ten programs in the nation wanted me. I thought this would be easy, but it was actually the most difficult decision that I had to make.

"Wait, so why did you bring me here for this.?" That's when Fred smiled.

"When you were about seven months, your daddy saw you pulling something in his house. He was on the phone with me and said my son gone be a football player. I wanna be there when he opens his letters. Your mom in Newport sent 'em to the house. You gotta helluva lot more, but she thought these three were the big ones."

Now I see what my purpose was. Now I know who the dark figure in my dream was. More importantly, I know why I seen my name on that headstone. Something had to die inside of me. At this moment, it was hatred. When I started to walk away from my father's gravesite, it was out of hatred that his lifestyle led to his demise before I had the chance to even start a relationship with him. Now, out of my heart grew forgiveness. I had nothing to be mad at him for. He wanted to see me open my first letter. Now, his wish had come true. I didn't know whether my father was in heaven or hell. What I did know is that he seen what he had always wanted to see and that was his son achieving the first part of his dream. I walked back to the car with Fred, preparing to enjoy my last night here with the people I considered family.

"Thanks pops," I whispered.

"Thank you." We got back to the crib about 9:30 after stopping at Mickey D's and getting nine Egg McMuffin sandwiches. I swear I didn't eat anything else there but that. I could eat those for days. Of course Tep took like four of em, seeing that his greedy behind ate any and everything in sight. Today would be spent packing and just being lazy as tomorrow we would all go our separate ways again. I truly had enjoyed this trip, even if some of the instances left a bad taste in my mouth. It was about 11:00 when my phone rang. It was my mom.

Me: Hey mom!"
Mom: "Baby cakes! Guess What! Oregon just called. They want you and want you bad in Eugene!"

I'll be damned I thought. Now, things were just getting tougher. I thought my decision was a lock, but the lure of national championships and certain environments were taking me on a head spin. I had one more year in high school and I didn't wanna jump too soon. Plus, when I started to think about it, Sparty and crew were doing well, so I know that the recruiting class would be stacked. I wanted to be at a powerhouse, yet somewhere where I would serve an immediate impact. Education was the most important goal, but football was damn well up there with it. I finished up the convo with my moms and continued packing.

"A Ramses," Tep said as he was also packing.

"When we leave here bruh, this may be the last time we see each other." I stopped doing what I was doing.

"Man look. We brothers. Whenever you need me. I'll be there. It ain't no black, white, light, brown issue. We family. This wasn't random bruh. This was ordained. I love you mane." I dapped my brother up.

124

"I love you too big dawg. Who knows. Maybe I'll try out for football my senior year, make it and have an alternative to basketball. I ain't never put on pads in my life, but at 6'3, I think I'm good." I smiled at him.

"Hey man. I never thought I could be cold hearted and pull a trigger, but I did. It's nothing to be proud of, but I'm hoping God will forgive me."

"He will bruh," Tep responded.

"Lets finish this up so I can bust you up one mo' time on the basketball court." He knows those were fighting words. All the time we were here, it was primarily horse. We got like three one on ones, but it was nothing crucial. Tonight though, I was gonna ball him up like OJ Mayo was doing cats at USC. Just then, a knock was heard on the door.

"Come in," we said in unison. It was Fred.

"I hear y'all talking mess about who gone do what on the court. One last challenge for y'all tonight."

"C'mon Mr. taylor," Tep said.

"Man look, I ain't trying to be in no more episodes of the wild wild west." Mr. Taylor started laughing hysterically.

"I feel you. I feel you. However, that ain't what I'm talking about. Y'all two have done everything together except for fight yourselves." We looked at each other confused as hell as to what Mr. Taylor was saying.

"What you mean fight?," I asked him.

"Just like I said. Fight. Tonight's your last night. In my hand, I got the key to both of y'all lives. Now both of y'all are probably thinking what in the good hell is he talkin' about. If you seen he got game, Jesus played his father. If his pops won, he went to Big State. If he loss, Jesus could do whatever. Tonight, y'all are against each other. One of you is 6'1, 210 and can hit someone like a Mack truck. The other one of you is 6'3, 190 and prides himself on finesse. Whoever wants it, you gonna earn it. Meet at the truck. Six o'clock tonight. We going to play under the lights. One game. One shot. To 15, by twos and ones. The winner has his life changed forever. The loser, has his life changed forever. Y'all down?" We once again stared at each other. This time though, Tep looks changed to one I had never seen. He had a demeanor on his face that said here we go again.

"I'm down," I said as I looked at Tep.

"Same here Mr. Taylor," as Tep mugged me down as he walked out the room. Here we were, pitted against each other once again, about to battle this time for something neither one of us knew. Tep was out back shooting hoops, vigorously practicing his moves. As for me, I relaxed in the house and watched TV with a warm sausage and mushroom pizza at my disposal. Mr. Taylor was out working on his wife's car while she was outside doing yard work. We were all separated in our own worlds. As I continued to watch TV, I saw a Bible on the bookshelf. During commercial, I got up, grabbed it, came back to sit down and flipped it to a random page. I landed in the book of Deuteronomy. I decided what the heck and just decided to read the whole book. As I delved deep into the reading, once verse in one chapter stuck out more than any other to me. It was Deuteronomy, chapter 28, verse 39. And it read: *"You will plant vineyards and cultivate them but you will not drink the wine or gather the grapes."*

I thought it was the most retarded thing that I had ever read. Like, I ain't callin' God retarded by any means. However, what man is gonna plant vineyards and cultivate them, but not get to drink his own wine. That is almost as crazy as the people who yell that you can't have your cake and eat it too. Why the hell can't I have some cake if it's my damn cake? I got up and put The Bible back on the shelf because I felt that it was trippin'. I continued to indulge in myself along with everyone else and just wait until the time rolled around for me to do what I had to do. That, simply was win.

6 BLACK ON BLACK

Trinidad Slaves (All Controlled Everything)

I wasn't born with a silver spoon, I was born with a golden tongue, my biggest tool and my worst enemy, at times it's a friend of me, other times it speaks death into me, but most importantly, it speaks life and strife, see they say never bring a knife to a gunfight, but they aint never tell you that the guns don't fight, they just release, its people who fight and beef, making the gun an accessories to their misgivings, cause giving slugs for bad drugs is the new norm,

while our homes become worn down, and our walls speak the sounds of gun clapping and fiends yappin, ratchet is now the new classy and being smart is the new dumb, so I guess I'm one of the dumbest men you can find, because I questioned the times we live in, when people can paste pics on sites of a murder like its funny, so maybe thats why the government laugh at us when they kill us with man made diseases and infect your food with pesticides, no fear, knowing the only repercussion that they'll face are picture slides with the words "genetically altered their food and U.O.E.N.O. it," and the problem is we do know it, yet most sit back and don't wanna face the facts, they'd rather listen to the raps, where they tell you popped the molly Im sweatin...woo....and the gov't spit they own song with "killin em slowly we flexin...woo, got the country in chains.....wall street money rings.....enslavement comin just watch......don't believe us just watch...nigga, nigga, niggas, and mexicans, and whites, and ricans, and for all who aint believin in what they tell you, watch how quick you get shot down, watch how chopper rounds turn you from American to terrorist threat, yet don't fret, cause we'll still have the BET awards, we'll still have men dressed like women, women hating men yet wanting to look like one and most of all, we'll have that chip in the right hand, tracking you across the land, and if your scan aint right, your shelf life is revoked, because the purchase of your soul is how they plan to take control

It was 6:05. For the first time since I been here, me and Tep were in separate cars. Whatever it was that we would battle it out on the court for, it must have been beyond important if they didn't even want us to be together. I rode with Fred's wife.

"Mrs. Taylor?"

"Nope, nope, nope. Focus. Don't ask me nothing." She obviously knew how important this was as well seeing that she didn't even want me talking. I took in my last night in Alabama as a classic one. All eyes were on me and for what, I had no idea. We ended up back in Ensley. Flashbacks of everything occurred as I tried to focus. I kept seeing Gold Mouth and hundreds of guns, however. I shook it off as much as I could. We hit the bend on another block and ended up at a park. I saw Fred's truck parked and Tep already outside on the court shooting.

I also saw a crowd gathered. This was some Hollywood type stuff. Here we are in the middle of the hood, lights on at the basketball court, with two brothers who were about to give it their all for something that neither one of us knew. Once we parked, I got out, game time ready. I walked inside the cage to the sight of Gold Mouth, his goons and a bunch of other brothers that I didn't know. Tep immediately stopped shooting and stared me down. Basketball was his life and I know he did not like to lose, seeing that he already won one state title in Oregon as a freshman. I walked to mid-court and just stood there, mugging Tep. The smell of weed smoke was actually appalling, as I didn't like it at all. However, trying to play the hard role, I inhaled it with every whiff I caught.

"Come over here Tep," Fred yelled. He walked and met me at mid court, getting within two inches of my face. I ain't like nobody this close in my bubble, but I would let it slide this one time.

"AIGHT YOU ALL!," Fred yelled. "HERE WE ARE! THEIR LAST NIGHT HERE IN B-HAM! THEIR LAST NIGHT IN BAMA! Y'ALL DONE DID EVERYTHING HERE EXCEPT SHOOT THE WAR EAGLE, WHICH WE ALL HATE! NOW, Y'ALL GOT ONE FINAL CHALLENGE! Y'ALLSELVES! GAME 15, BY ONES AND TWOS. THE WINNER GETS WHAT'S IN THIS BOX. RAMSES, YOU GET FIRST BALL. MAKE IT, TAKE IT! LET THE GAMES BEGIN FELLAS!" Fred slammed the ball in my stomach and backed off towards the sidelines.

"Lemme see what you made of Newport!," Gold Mouth yelled. The crowd on the sideline was getting amped. The talk, the chatter, all that had begun. I held on to the ball not even knowing that I was holding on to the ball. That's how much in awe I was.

"You gone check the rock or hold it like a lil bitch?" I looked up at Tep not knowing who in the good hell he was talking too. Those were fighting words in my eyes.

"Check bitch!," as I flung the ball at him. He flung it back. I immediately used my strength, which was my physical strength and dribbled damn near through him. I gave him the Jordan push off at his waist, stepped back and fired from behind the arc. Two points down, 13 to go.

"Just like Jordan bitch. Go get my rock!" Oh I know I pissed him off them. Not to mention everyone on the court heard me. Tep furiously went and got the ball, tossing it back at me. I knew he wasn't gonna let me body him like that all game, so I immediately started to think of my next move. I brought the ball out, but he kept a good distance in front of me.

"Shoot again, I dare you. Just know if you miss, it's game over." He was leaving me room, daring me to shoot it. Me being me, I launched up another one from behind the arc. Swiss! 4-0. This time, I left my hand up like I was J bone on Byron Russell.

"Do you want mo'!," I asked him. He was furious now and it didn't do well for him that the sidelines were eggin' me on. I got the ball back and went right, but he stripped me. I reached in to try and get it back, but I slipped. As I lie on the ground, I watched him run and take off, doing a reverse slam. The sideline went crazy as he came back down to earth, grabbin the ball, walking over an placing it in my chest.

"First point of 15 lil man. Check rock!" I shoved the ball back at him. He threw it back. I threw it right back. He was now laughing. I had to take him out of his zone. He had me backin' up. I can't lie, the boy had handles. He looked damn near like Chef Curry. As he put a cross move on me, I stayed with him. He brought it back so quickly that it left me amazed. As he began to go forward, he stopped and I continued to back trek. He stepped back behind the arc. Swoosh.

"4-3 lil man. This what yall do in Cali?" I was furious. I

went and got the ball and carried it back in his face.

"Only thing we do in Cali is run the coast. Don't nobody give a damn 'bout no Oregon. Yall got more trees than people." I shot the ball back at him. I got aggressive, hand checking him with the hardest of hand checks you could ever imagine.

"Get off me" he was yelling while he tried to drive. He started to cross, but I stripped him. He slipped as he tried to regain balance, but it was too late. I drove to the hole for an easy layup. 5-3. As I went to check back up, the look in his eyes started to change. I now found Tep's weakness. As good as he was, he was not comfortable being down. More so, he was not comfortable when being down in front of a crowd. He felt like he had to prove something, especially with his skin color. I can only imagine as I drifted into another zone. Then, I went from imagining to relating. Up there, he was the only brother on his team, in a city where its 85% white. In Newport, I was one of four black people on the football team and I went both ways on the field. We were the minority and I indeed felt what he felt.

"C'mon man! Dribble the damn ball." Right then and there, I looked over at Fred, Gold Mouth and the rest of the cats on the sideline. Then, the reality of the situation hit me. Just like Denzel in the prison yard, I chucked the ball over the cage. Everyone all of a sudden got quiet. I walked over about five feet in front of Fred.

"I know what you doing. You showed me so much since I been here that I lost track of what was really going on. Look at everyone out here with you. They family. Me and Tep, we family. This whole time you were pitting me against family, but I forgot the biggest lesson. You never go against family. If something pops off, you can discuss right or wrong later, but you never go against family. Sorry Fred for my French, but fuck this game. That ball don't come between us. You know what I realized most of all? It's that we all niggas. No matter how good or bad we do, we all niggas to this world. So fuck it. If I'm gone be labeled a nigga by this fucked up world, then best believe I ain't gone war with my nigga." All of a sudden things got quiet. The whole sidelines started to walk on the court and circle up around me. Tep was still at mid-court dumbfounded as to what was going on. Gold Mouth came dead in my face and just stared at me. That's when Tep came breaking through the wall of people and jumped right by my side.

"I don't know what y'all got planned, but you swing at him, I'm swingin' at you. Fuck if we die. I'd rather die fighting than on my knees like a bitch."

"WHAT ABOUT ME?!," one of Gold's 300 plus pound goons said as he ran up in Tep's face.

"What if I swing on you?!" "Then you better be ready to go to hell with me big boy. 'Cause if you think this skinny frame ain't packing a punch you'z bout as dumb as the person who made your college logo an elephant." Hot damn, I honestly thought Tep was dead. That's when Fred stepped in between everybody. "Lemme tell y'all both something," carrying the box in his hand.

"Look?" He opened it up. It wasn't nothing in it.

"I thought you would've got it before, but it took you damn near beating each other to death to see it. Nothing and I mean nothing comes between family. I knew you two wouldn't get it. Tep, you pride yourself on proving everybody wrong that you'll jump into any situation head first just to show that you'll do it. Ramses, once you in a fight, you start to think. But tell me, who thinks when they are in actual combat? Ain't no timeout to think once the war starts. The thinking fool gets killed. Once you in battle, you battle. Y'all gotta see this about y'all selves if y'all gone do it. You see Gold Mouth, Lo, me and everyone else here. Some on the good side of the law, some on the wrong side. But the one thing that is the common denominator is that we all family. At the end of the day, the same blood running through my veins runs through theirs. Lemme tell you something. You don't let nothing, and I mean NOTHING, EVER, break the family apart. That's yo' last lesson." We then stood there under the lights, not saying a word to each other. It was an eerie silence. It stayed that way until Tep dapped up big Lo and "all was one" once again. Everyone then came in, dapping us up, showing us love. As Gold Mouth showed love, he whispered something in my ear.

"A, don't tell 'em I told you this. You was Jordan and he was Kobe. You were the master teaching the student." I laughed at cuz, 'cause I couldn't think of nothing else to do. The lesson was learned. The journey was complete. I was now more than a man. I was a man on my own path. My book was always right. I just confused the chapters of it. I think Tep confused his as well. His book was the same. His chapters were just screwed and chopped based on his mindset of showing and proving everyone wrong. In theory, his story should have always been to prove to God and himself. We stayed on that court for quite a while that night, embracing family and all becoming connected. I don't know if there will ever be a next time in Alabama. I don't know if there will be a next time in Birmingham. What I do know, is that there would be a next time with my life. I was grateful and no one could take this experience away from me ever.

We got to the center Friday morning at eight o'clock. All the heads who set this up would be coming in at around 8:45 a.m. to get the final analysis from all the students who took part in this. It didn't feel right being with my classmates again. It was just something about the fam that I had met out here.

"Yo man what's good?!" That was Carlos running over to

me.

"Man what crazy stuff they have you doing over these two weeks mane?"

"I learned about me man."

"I'm glad you did man, cause I ain't learn nothing except what not to be. Man you know we ain't do nothing meaningful at all. All we did was go to these youth centers and talk to kids who already had it made. I-I-I couldn't rock with this man. I'm from the O-A-K. I thought I was gone meet some cats like me. You know, help them out so they wouldn't be nine years old getting shot at. This here man. Never again. I see most these folks did this to make themselves look good. In truth, they aint give a damn about our struggle. It don't change bruh. No matter if you poor and black, or rich and black, they could careless about the struggle. I'll never do this again, but I'm glad I did it."

"Why is that?," I asked.

"Simple. Because now I know what a two faced human being looks like." We stared at each other for a minute. I wanted to tell him my story, but the timing wasn't right. This dude had just dropped a bomb. Now, I was upset. I didn't know anything else any one of us experienced, but seeing the looks on their faces, it didn't look like anything life altering. I seen Ms. Dockery make her way into the room with Mr. Lile.

"Good morning all. Parents, educators and students. Over these last two weeks, you have learned the true meaning of what it is to help others. Does anyone wanna share their experience?" One by one, students started raising their hands, giving these tails of community centers and baseball games in other affluent neighborhoods. Me and Carlos just shook our heads. When I looked across the room to Tep, I saw that he was feeling the same way, as he shook his head in utter disbelief at what he was hearing. I was hoping like hell she would call on me, but I knew she wasn't. This was what we called "coons" in the black community. Now let me explain this, because many people have this misconception that a coon is someone who doesn't agree with the majority of our people. That is not the case. A coon is someone who purposely ignores their own blackness and tries to shun us out, all for the sole purpose of appeasing others. That is a coon. She indeed was one. If I had black paint to put across her eyes, I most certainly would. We sat back listening to BS stories for the next 45 minutes. We were all slated to be out of here at 12, on our way to the airport to go back to our respective homes. Once intermission occurred, myself and Carlos went over to Ms. Dockery and Mr. Lile as they both engaged in a conversation.

"Excuse me Ms. Dockery. Can I ask you something?" With a stern look on her face, she said sure.

"All I wanna know is this. Why did you bring all of us out here, explaining that we were here for the less fortunate, and all you did was parade them around kids who had their lives made? I mean, the way I see it is that you aint nothing but a hypocrite."

"Excuse me young man?"

"He said you're a hypocrite, and I agree," Carlos added on. "You do know that I wasn't born and raised in Newport. I only went there when me daddy hit it big when I was 15. I'm straight no filter, Oakland born and raised. East Oakland that is. Right off Seminary, aka the cemetery. You see, my golds in my mouth ain't going nowhere. My dreads ain't going nowhere. Oh sure, you looked at us and thought why do we have a few colored niggas on this trip. Yes, I said colored!" By this time, Carlos voice was raising and the people in the general area who could hear the conversation started to turn their attention to where we were at. "You probably still call yourself colored. Well guess what. I was proud of how I came up. I grew up with hustlas, killas, drug dealers, all that. As you can see, I'm still a 3.7, B average student with an IQ that's higher than anything you ever had in life. This wasn't no attempt to help the fuckin' poor. This was your false attempt to make the melanin in your skin disappear. There ain't nothing you can tell me about being black."

"**LET ME TELL YOU TWO NIGGERISH BASTARDS SOMETHING!!!**" The whole place got quiet as a mouse. She looked around as if she accidently spewed those words out of her mouth. She knew damn well she meant it and she for surely knew that she messed up big time.

"You don't gotta tell us nothing Ms. Dockery. You just answered our question for us." Carlos walked away after saying that and I followed right behind. All these other folks didn't know what happened. I seen Fred off in the corner with his wife as we walked back to the other side of the building to get some chill. He nodded his head at me as if to say,

"that's how you stand up for your people." I knew what we had just did would probably get us banned for any future school trips or whatever, but we really didn't care. I had finally embraced the most important lesson that I had learned while down here. That lesson was to embrace that skin tone in which we call black. We ended up outside, blowing off some steam. Tep came out the doors soon after.

"Yo Ram? That shit. That shit you and ya mans just did. 100."

"Tep my dude, this Carlos mane." They shook up. "Pleasure to meet another brother. So I hear you was with my mans out there hittin' a few licks."

"Yeah. Yeah. I was with my brothers learning lessons in life. Whether good or bad, I'll never turn my back on family." We all clicked in that moment, becoming one as a unit. As the hours passed, we spent our time choppin' it up. Then, it was time to bounce. We exchanged numbers and everyone started to go their separate ways.

"If you ever in Portland, just know that 5-3 lead aint permanent." I laughed at my bro.

"You just remember to be catching football passes next year so you can join me at Michigan State."

"We'll see bruh. We'll see." I dapped my brother up one last time and we hugged that brother hug that only brothers do." With a dap of Carlos and a deuce sign, he was on his way to the bus to head back to Portland to continue his life. Our bus pulled up shortly after his. As we began to board, Mr. Lile stopped me outside of the bus.

"Ramses. As a man. I tell you the truth. I didn't care much when I got here. Hell, I didn't even understand a lot about anyone who didn't have as much as me. Umm....what I'm trying to say is that I was very impressed with how you handled that back there. So I just wanted to tell you before we started on the trip back that I'm sorry." Mr. Lile extended his hand. I shook it and smiled, but I hit him with lasting words.

"Well sir. The one you need to apologize to isn't me. It's the one you look at in the mirror. That's the one you failed." I threw him a quick smirk and got on the bus. Carlos was right in the front. I sat next to him, asking him why the hell he sat up so close to the driver.

"Hell after those two weeks, I'm bout to make Rosa Parks proud. I'm sitting in the front." I dapped my dude up and we were on our way to the airport. The flight was a smooth one. Four hours and some change, and we were landing back in L.A. on a Friday. I still had a whole weekend ahead of me. My mom was there to greet me as soon as I made it to baggage claim. She was so ecstatic, especially seeing that she had a bag full of college letters for me. It was amazing to be back home. However, I felt like a piece of me was left in Birmingham. I started to feel like I had been there my whole life and that this place was new.

"What do you wanna do Ram? Get some ice cream with

mama?"

"Naw ma. I just wanna go home. I just wanna go home and be a family for this weekend. I missed you." She gave me that motherly kiss on the cheek that all boys hated to get, especially in public at this age. Especially in L.A. where there were pretty girls always walking around. Someone probably thought I had caught me a cougar. We made it to the car after God knows how long in this crowded mecca. It felt good to just smell California. The palm trees and the terrible drivers had me feeling like I was in heaven. It would be a while before I got home. Newport wasn't that far, but L.A. kept a traffic jam on deck. This was the only city where it could be nine o'clock at night and traffic would still be backed up for miles on a freeway. Truthfully, I didn't care this time. I just wanted to get to the comforts of the crib. After about an hour on the road and a few middle fingers my mama threw up, we made it. Here I was, back in Ritzyville, U.S.A.

"Son welcome home." That was pops greeting me as soon as I came to the door.

"I wanna hear all about the trip." I literally dropped my bags and plopped on the couch.

"Trust me dad, mom. Y'all don't wanna know about the trip that I had."

"Serious son, I do. I think your mama agrees," as she sat there shaking her head up and down so happily. "Well....I shot someone. I saw a dead body. I saw someone get killed. I seen more cocaine than Tony Montana ever sniffed. I cursed out the old lady who was with us. That's the trip in a nutshell." They looked at each other with a weird look. Then they burst out laughing.

"Nice one Ram. Giving us that wild wild west story. Now really, what happened." I knew they wouldn't believe it. I told them a watered down version of everything. I lied for the most part. They weren't ready for the truth. Sometimes, as hard as it may be, we gotta lie. I know God says don't lie, but you absolutely have to sometimes. We know ordinary kids can't be the president. It's a bloodline that is kept tight. The President of the United States of America is selected before they are elected. However, if a kid asks can they be the president, you tell them yes you can. Some things in life you just have to face the consequences of your word at a later time.

We talked for almost three hours in the living room, sipping some of my mom's homemade grape juice throughout the conversation. I swear this stuff was so good that it could make a bull buck without having a shock on his nuts. As it got a little bit past six, I headed off to my room to just relax. There was a cool breeze tonight, so I opened up my window and just felt a rush of relief. Life was indeed back to normal. The beach air and the sight of crashing waves gave me a peace that I hadn't had in two weeks. Actually, it made me think about how peaceful the last two weeks were. When we usually go through adverse situations, we find ourselves at war with our minds. We think in our heads that the world is falling apart when in actuality, it may be all coming together. Wrapping my mind around the lesson that I learned, it gave me peace. Notice I said lessons and not the cause of those lessons. I wouldn't do what I did down there ever again, but at least I learned about myself. That, in itself brought me peace. Peace of mind will always be bigger than a piece of money. Money can't buy you happiness, as you can see with the wealthiest of people always killing themselves. I stayed cooped up in here for a good hour, lying down on the bed until moms knocked at my door.

"You have a visitor Ramses!" I sat up on the bed wondering who in the good hell is visiting me on my first day back. She opened the door up and there was Carlos.

"Wassup bro!," as he walked in.

"Thanks mom. Yo wassup partna."

"Yo man look. I got the car tonight. Pops proud of the work I did out there, so he let me be on cruise control for the night."

"Work, man you told me you didn't do any meaningful work out there."

"Then what you call going off on Mrs. Dockery, letting her know that she is as black as the North Pole. He called her and lit into her man." I couldn't do anything but laugh as I dapped my boy up. We headed downstairs and indulged in a homemade pizza that moms had cooked. She knew how much I loved sausage and mushrooms on a pizza, and moms always kept me happy. Once we finished the last slice. It was time to get it in with my partner on this Friday night.

"Mom, is it okay if we head out for a good while?"

"ENJOY YOUR SPRING BREAK RAM BAM! I TRUST YOUR DECISIONS!," she shouted from the other room.

"Ram Bam," Carlos whispered. "You mama call you Ram Bam?"

"I'm gone call you mush face if you don't walk out the door and stop roasting." We laughed as we headed out to the car. We got out into the night time breeze just chillin, doing what two young brothers do. That was enjoy life. For like the first thirty minutes, we just drove around, talking about everything that went down back in Alabama. We took it on down by the mall across from The Island Hotel and Resort. True, out here, malls weren't malls like you seen in the city. It wasn't any urban spot where you could go get fresh at out here. That was LA, Ontario, places like that. The mall here was different than the rest. It was just restaurants and high end joints. Not to mention the humans carrying dogs and the babies walking around on a leash. It was ass backwards and I didn't wanna hear any more about Adrian Peterson whoopin' a child. If this wasn't coined child abuse, something was seriously wrong with this country. We walked around stopping in random stores, not buying anything. We saw all the usual high profile people that we usually seen around here....which were porn stars. It was crazy that they could be the wildest acting bunch of folks on camera, but when you see them out in public they were the most normal dressed and normal acting people you could ever encounter. It was odd, but it was the truth. We finished up round here a lil bit after 8:30 and headed down to the coast, where all the nightclubs and everything were. We were way too young to get in, but looking at all the college girls who were here on spring break had our heads spinning. Living out here, I had a thing for white girls. I didn't discriminate at all. All vaginas were pink in my eyes no matter what skin tone it was attached too. I lost my virginity to a white chick. I'm pretty sure that I would slay some more the longer I was out here.

This experience had me wanting to grow up faster than what I wanted too, I couldn't even lie. I was ready for the college life. I was hoping that my senior year in high school would fly by with the quickness. Then, I thought about it. I really didn't want it to end. High school was the mecca. It was the last time you could be looked on as a God simply because you did things on the sports field. It was the last time that being popular could actually carry you far. Once you hit the real world, all that was done and over with.

"A bruh?," I asked Carlos. "Like really. What you wanna do with yo life when you leave after next year?" He stayed quiet for a minute as we cruised.

"I dunno mane. I never really thought about it. I mean, going back to the hood to help those would be nice. You know, like a counselor of some sorts to inner city youth. Lord knows I needed them. But you need college for that, and right now, I don't know if I wanna deal with another four years of higher education. What about you?" I pondered for a minute as I watched a group of bangin' white girls across the street as we were at the light.

"Man, as crazy as it may sound, I wanna be a spoken word artist. You know, put poetry and motivational speaking together."

"Oh yea, you wanna be one of those roses are red, violets are blue type niggas huh?" He started laughing, but I was dead serious. "Man, you ain't joking is you?," as he looked at me before heading through the now green light.

"Naw man. I mean, I've always had the gift of gab. I always had the right words to help the next man get through his situation, whatever it may be. I dunno man. I don't want any old 9 to 5. I don't want that shit at all. I wanna be my own independent operator. I want people to pay me for simply talking. Like, real shit." He nodded his head up and down as Mac Dre blazed through the speakers.

"Well, my dude. Its only one thing I can say about your dream. Just remember. Before you live your dream, you just might have to live someone else's. It may not come in the time you want it, but if you put the right effort into it, oh my dude you got it. Just like I'm about to get this burger from the malt shop real quick if we can find a place to park."

Those words etched into my cranial something serious. The whole living someone else's dream before living yours. I never even looked at it in that manner. I was so focused on just doing me, that I failed to realize that I had to take baby steps. Hell, even Jesus had to get tested on numerous occasions before He fulfilled the purpose of His Father. We finally got a parking spot and walked back down two blocks to the malt shop. As we sat down mashing some peanut butter shakes while waiting for our burgers, we started to look at our lives a whole different way. We got into talking about how no matter what our dreams were, we eventually wanted to become businessmen. We wanted to escape the 9 to 5 world and have the world as our 9 to 5. You know it's crazy. I once read that slave owners were once 5% of the population of America and the other 95% were slaves. Now, in modern times, that stat is still the same, except it's been transferred over to the workforce. Only this time, no race, creed or color was spared. 5% of the people make the money and the other 95% made sure the 5% made the money. Sure, you will always have to start somewhere, but if you're not striving to lead yourself and set your family up for success, then you're failing yourself. We saw how Newport operated. Most people out here were either retired or business owners. If they did have a 9 to 5, it was something that was a necessity like doctors or other highly sought professionalist. That's the life that we seen. That's the life that we wanted. That's the life that we strived for.

"Dawg, let's go back to Alabama?" Carlos stopped indulging in that milkshake and looked at me strange.

"Man is you crazy? Don't get me wrong, it's cool, but that place ain't for me."

"Naw man like, I mean, really, like I see big things down there with those people."

"My nigga. You stayed on the Southside, in the rich part. You seen the hood. You shot some bullets. You seen some drugs. Congrats, you got the hood experience, but it don't make you hood my nigga." I was taken back at his tone and demeanor. It was like I offended him or something.

"Look man, I ain't saying that. I'm just saying man that we can work down there and help 'em man. I mean, everyone gotta start somewhere and it's people like us responsibility to help em out."

"Naw nigga. You help 'em out. Nigga I been there, done that. You think anyone helped my pops? You think niggas was knocking on the door saying here man, here go some shoes for school. Or here goes so food so yall can eat. Hell nah.

Niggas is out for they selves in the hood. Niggas slang a little dope and what they get. Cars, jewelry, shit like that. Nigga they ain't caring 'bout no niggas except maybe they grandma. You make it out and all of a sudden the whole damn hood think that you supposed to take them with you, like you are a free ass cab ride or some shit. My dad saw the same thing when he made a way for me and my moms. Everybody wanted a piece of the pie and didn't buy an ingredient to put in that muthafucka. And you think I'm going back around that? Hell nah. People gone look at it as I forgot where I came from. Naw, never that. I'm an Oakland nigga till I die. If I got my choice, they gone bury me under the blocks themselves. But why, why would I go resort back in a place where the negative stays negative? You gotta think about that man. You aint never experienced it so I understand. But it's gone be even worse being an outsider from Cashville, U.S.A. and think you gone go in there and change their minds. They gone look at you like another rich man trying to flaunt in their face and you might get muffed. Think bout that bro. Think about it. You can't help anyone who aint willing to help themselves." When he put it in that perspective, I really had to ponder on the idea. I wanted to leave a remarkable mark on this world. I also wanted to give back. The crazy thing is, though, is that I knew I could do it.

"I'm doing it bro. I appreciate the words of wisdom, but I'm gone do it."

"Aight nigga. You gone learn the hard way. But let me ask you this. Since your heart is so set on being that type of person, which by the way, I am not knocking at all. **BUT!** What do you plan on doing for Birmingham or any other poverty stricken hood that you encounter?" I don't know why he asked that because it was simple in my eyes.

"I'm gonna give back man. Give those people something that they never had. That's called a chance. They never had a chance. I'm gonna give them that." Carlos looked at me while sippin' the end of that milkshake to the point he was making that irritating noise when nothing was left in the cup. Our food came, he took one bite into that burger and the convo continued.

"So," talking with his mouth full.

"Shit that was good. So listen to what you just said. You wanna give back. That's the damn problem with all of the niggas who make it out the hood right now. They wanna give back."

"How is that a problem my dude?," I asked him, cause I wasn't getting what he was tryna get at.

"Look, they program everyone who makes it out to give back. Thanksgiving comes around and someone gives out turkey dinners. Christmas comes around and someone gives out presents. A football star or a basketball star comes back and they give these kids a camp in the same sport they excelled in. Failing to mention to all of those youngsters that only maybe one of them in that room will reach the NFL, NBA, MLB or whatever other sports. How many niggas you hear come back and teach these kids something? How many of 'em go back and have a day to just teach a kid how to tie a tie.

I mean, you're gonna have to start in the workforce before you can hopefully one day be the man. You know how many grown ass men cant tie a tie? Why don't someone come back and teach how to fit a well tailored suit. Why don't someone come back and teach how to write a resume or a presentation? Write a damn 100 word essay, cause lets face it. Niggas from where I'm from, especially Castle school niggas, couldn't write shit. I was damn near a God when I was up there. Making money to write niggas book reports. How many people come back and teach untiy? How many people come back and teach niggas how to read credit reports? I know damn well I ain't have that. See," as he took another bite into that mushroom and swiss burger. "Mofos happy with just seeing those cats in the hood. They wanna say my nigga still come back. He ain't forgot where he came from. He still be in the hood like he never left. Niggas is so programmed to rap music that they think that is all to be done. I know I'm rambling for a long time but here me out. When Huey P. and The Panthers were up there well before I was born, they not only helped the community, but they taught them as well. That's the real reason the government was so adamant and still is to this day about destroying the black man. You give a black man a stage and he is no threat. You give him a stage, an audience, a mic, with the ability to instill black pride in his peoples, and then you have public enemy number one. So really. What you wanna do? Give back to get a pat on the back. Or, do you wanna really teach these people how to make it? I ain't a Bible thumper, but I think JC said give a nigga a fish and he can eat for a day. Teach that nigga how to hook them muthafuckas,and he'll be having lifetime fish fries. All he gotta do is have someone bring the side dishes."

By this time, he was licking the sauce off his fingers as he devoured his burger in the midst of giving me the "By Any Means Necessary' speech part 2. Me on the other hand, my food had just sat there. It was cold to death, much like the words my dude just told me.

"You gone eat man? Cause I don't like to see some good ass meat go to waste?"

"Yea I'mma take it with me. Let's pay this bill and roll man." Carlos got up to go to the bathroom. The waitress came over and gave me my bill.

"Do you need a doggy bag sir?"

"Yes please."

"Hope you're okay. You sound down." As she departed, I followed her with my eyes to the back. She was indeed a cutie. Puerto Rican at that. I hadn't seen a Rican sister here since I first dropped down. I shook that off quick, though. I didn't need to be thinkin' about a girl at this time and hour. I had bigger fish to fry on my stove.

"Here you go, cutie." She smiled and walked away, turning back to look at me as she headed back behind the counter. I was struck. I know she was just hoping that I would go back over and ask her for her number, but my deep thought ass blew it. I simply went to the front register, paid for my meal and walked outside.

"Nigga I seen that. Did you get her number?," as Carlos met me outside of the door.

"Naw man. My focus is in other places.

"Man if you don't take yo brown skinned, Shemar Moore lookin ass back in there and get that. How many bad ass Rican sisters you see round here? Nigga." He literally pushed me back into the malt shop until we seen her. He then looked at her, pointing at me while mouthing something and walked off. I was so nervous as she was walking up.

"So you a lil shy I see?"

"Naw...I mean...like.........I'm Ramses." We shook hands as she stared at me weird.

"Ramses? Yo mama named you Ramses?" She got a good laugh out of that.

"Well, what's yours?"

"Renae." She luckily was on break and we ended up talking for fifteen minutes. I don't know what Carlos was doing, but he became irrelevant to me. She was from nearby Laguna Beach and was also a junior in high school. We exchanged numbers and I went back outside. I saw Carlos sitting on the bench outside playing on his phone.

"Well did you get the number?" I just held up my phone.

"Well good, cause I was gonna slap the hell outta you if you didn't. That one was too fine too pass up. Let's roll man." We got back to the car and continued on with the night. We headed back down the coast and just rocked out to Wale. As the drive went along, I saw my life outside the window. I saw the life that I had been accustomed too. I saw what I needed to do next.

"Stop the car bruh." Carlos pulled over to the side of the road.

"Sup?"

"You know how when we get back to school.....and we gotta give a report or a speech on what we experienced?"

"Yea, what about it?"

"I just found my revelation big dog. Wait 'til Tuesday in Mrs. Kraylin class."

"Nigga I don't got Mrs. Kraylin," he told me.

"Well come in at 9:30. What I'm gone tell about Birmingham and us in general is big." He looked at me up and down.

"Well look who tapping into his inner blackness. Right Book, Wrong Chapter." I whipped my head around at him.

"Right Book, Wrong Chapter? Man what you talking about?" He started to laugh as he pulled off.

"You ain't never read that joint I see? It was never no big seller or all world book. But it was a lesson in what you are. My daddy had a copy of that shit back in the Bay. Hell he still got it on his bookshelf now that I think about it. It was written by an old slave I believe, but I really don't know. In one part, she talks about finding your inner blackness. Yea, we all black, but does your blackness only go skin deep or does it travels through your arteries?" Things got silent as he hit the light.

"Yea, you forgot I was raised off Huey's logic something hard. It's Oakland my nigga. It's forever in me." I knew then what was about to go down.

7 WHEN THE NIGGA EMERGES

B.M.F (BLACK MAN FEARS)

They asked me what's the scariest thing to be in this world, I told em its simple, a black man, you aint gotta believe me, all you gotta do is ask Jesus, skin of bronze, hair of sheeps wool, and them folks acted a fool on him, slaughtered him on a cross with nails in his palms, and even though it was wrong, one thing relates to this situation, both our skins had the same pigmentation, now I know a lot of what happens is brought upon ourselves, but presently we are the ones on the back of the shelf, hidden from view as others shop and pick their way through America's system, while a lot of us eventually join it, and a lot of times its not due to our own faults, they need people to run the labor so more land can be bought and more prisons can get built, see being a black man is equivalent of walking on stilts, its an unbalanced life, one minute, we speaking on the streets, the next, we catching the beat in corporate America, the next, we bearing the weight of superstar status on basketball courts, football fields, and all sports that yield a profit, see we got it in many of ways, but at the end of the day, we still a nigger in most folks eyes, despised even if we put on the uniform to defend the stars and stripes, because our pride got swiped a long time ago, starting with the firehouse and the rotts, till modern day with the tasers from the cops, being black is like being a wanted convict, on the run twenty four seven, lookin at the heavens for that north star guidance, hoping we can make it through without getting beat on tape, or hung from a tree, see this poem aint a representation of me, its a representation of all of us, cause trust, anyone who black will tell you, its the scariest thing to encounter, its scary as hell where we come from, but to get to where we are going is like a damn nightmare that we trapped in for life, and sometimes, life in prison is the only escape, cause be institutionalized publicly, is sometimes better than being institutionalized secretly.

Class got back underway for me on Tuesday. I thought about everything that me and Carlos rapped about. I knew this group discussion class was gonna be different today. Matter fact, I knew it would change my life forever.

"Well let's clap it up for Mr. Alabama."

"Chris shut yo bitch ass up for I smack the fuck outta you." That mouth got quiet as he went back to his little rich kid smirk. I sat down at my desk and waited for Mrs. Kraylin to come in.

"How was the trip Ramses?," asked Brittany, the girl who sat behind me.

"Oh you'll see. Get ya popcorn. Group discussion will never be the same." Mrs. Kraylin finally came in.

"Alright class. Good morning. Today, I wanna switch things up. As you know, Ramses went on a community project down to Alabama for two weeks during spring break. So today, I'll let him explain what he experienced and we can discuss that.

You have the floor Ramses. I got up and proceeded to the middle of the class. As I did, a knock was at the door. I seen Carlos through the glass tellin me to open the door. I let him in.

"Sorry Mrs. Kraylin, but I couldn't miss what he is about to say. Do you mind?"

"No, not at all Carlos, but what hour are you in right now?"

"Art Mrs. Kraylin. I told Mr. Machuca I had to go take a number two." The whole class ewwed out.

"Man please. Actin like y'all rich tails don't shoot deuces. Hush up." Mrs. Kraylin was laughin' too hard.

"Alright Carlos. Enough talking about number two, shooting deuces or whatever you wanna call it. Go head Ramses." There I was. The floor was all mines. It was like everything got dark around me and the aura took effect. The class saw me as a normal human. I saw myself on a stage, with one spotlight on me, with an audience that i couldn't see. This was it. *"God, forgive 'em if they don't understand,"* I said to myself.

"So you ask me, Ramses? What do you mean when you title a speech "A Black Man has 9 Lives?" It is easy for me to simply answer that question for you. However, it will not be that simple. Ok, here is what I want you to do. I want you right now to stop at this point and take literally two minutes to think why I titled this speech that. I want you to think hard and think it through thoroughly." I literally shut up for two minutes. I wanted them to know the impact of what I was gonna say. Honestly, would they understand? I knew they wouldn't. They were rich white kids who never seen the other side. But hey, to educate is to teach.

"Ok, you should be done by now. Let me tell you exactly my motivation as to why I titled the speech this. When I get up every morning, I pass by one of my neighbors homes. Truthfully, I have never met these neighbors, nor have I seen them. For all I know, I am saying them when it could be just one person. I hope they forgive me if they ever find out that I said this. Anywho, 90% of the time as I pass by their living room window, their cat is either lying in a bed next to the window or it is sitting up in its bed, staring a hole through me as if I were a giant sized rat. As I thought one night on why this cat always stared at me, it popped in my head. A cat is an animal that they proclaim has nine lives. Hmmm? I wonder if I used that to think of an idea to speak about. Then, it hit me.

A black man has nine lives that he lives in his lifetime. Right now, some of you are scratching your head, wondering how in the hell does a black man have nine lives. Trust me, by the end of these words, you will truly realize what makes us such unique individuals. You may come to your own conclusions with what you hear. Some of you will strongly agree. Some of you will strongly disagree. Some of you will probably love me for saying what I am gonna say. Some of you will probably label me coon, Uncle Tom, sellout or whatever little terms you choose. You may even be calling me a nigger in your heads. However, keep that to yourself, cause I will bust you in the mouth. That's fine and dandy as well, however, as I know I could careless about the consequences. Too many, this is the introduction to Ramses Osiris Martin. I am simple. I am loud, brash, cocky at times, strongly opinionated, loud, yet humble and helpful. Unlike many who like to put on an alter ego for the public masses, you will not get an act from this individual. I am who I am. I have screwed up in more ways than one in my life. Shooting guns in public. Inappropriate actions to have me labeled of what I thought was right.

Financial mismanagement and drugs led to the death of my now deceased biological parents. Lying to people to ensure that they never knew who the real me was. Cheating myself and leading people on. Walking past homeless people with a wallet full of money and saying screw them because I was too concerned about them going to buy liquor. Saying mean things to people and being spiteful. Revenge minded, as I lived a lot of my life under the motto do worse to others than what they did to you. I don't even know if anyone has ever made that statement famous, but maybe I just did. That is just a small part of the flaws and mistakes that I have made throughout my short 16 years of life. It's easy for a man to sit up and boast about all the good things he has done in his life. It takes a real man to expose his dark side to the masses in hope that others who read his story will not make the same mistakes.

Now, I have done a lot of good, but those accomplishments are for The Good Lord and the people who I affected to know. I don't talk about that much, because as a human being, we should help each other when we have the chance. Could you even imagine if we all came together and actually lived as one? In that same sense, I want my black people to wonder what in the good hell would happen if we all came together? I can answer that right now. Unification and chaos. Ponder those two words and enjoy this read, as I take you on a ride inside the mind of an extraordinary gentlemen. Remember, extraordinary and basic thinking do not go together in the same sentence. If you are a basic thinker, then I suggest you to leave this class now, because this is not the speech for you."

"Birmingham. Ahhh, what can I say about Birmingham??? Actually, there are a million things I can say and tell you about the great city of Birmingham. I wasn't actually in Birmingham. I was in an entirely different world that was a 10–15 minute drive from Birmingham, Alabama that everyone who went was supposed to experience. Yea, I know what some of you are thinking. Well you all went down there helping the less fortunate people who live there. Hell nah. The same way a magician fools an audience. The same way that republicans and democrats are actually friends. Everything about that trip was simply deceiving. Furthermore, many of the people who went were down there to boost their own rich ass ego. We are one in the same? I think not. Hell, it was Alabama. I get that. It wasn't the rich, lavish life that we are accustomed to up here. But why minimize an experience because people aren't like you? We eat the same food, have the same love for sports teams, same attitudes, same mentalities when angry and overall, we both struggle. Birmingham is called The Magic City, but Newport needs to take that name, because this city and every other rich dummy city that was there disappeared, and it is truly sad. I remember when I actually went over to meet my sponsors and saw where they lived. Trust, it wasn't here, but it was damn sure the good life. Some things that I saw down there stuck out like a sore thumb." Just then, everything turned to the left.

"Look man?," as Chris jumped up out of his seat walking towards me. "No one cares. We're rich. Down there, it's just a bunch of what y'all call...**PO NIGGAS!!!**" Immediately I decked his bitch made ass and kept punching. As damn near the whole class pulled me off of him, I saw Carlos stompin' his face in something serious. I knew expulsion was possibly coming, but I didn't care. Rich and privileged didn't mean you had the right to down talk any man's race. Especially not mines. Don't care what city I'm in. You call me a nigga and I'm a show you a nigga. By the time all the smoke, dust and commotion cleared, school security were escorting me and Carlos out of the class and into their mini detention center.

"Fuck y'all gone do me like Oscar huh?! HUH?!" Carlos was furious and resisting as the police did their damnedest to contain him.

"**Fuck yall gone do man?!**" They did do something. As they were trying to calm him down, they sent him flying head first into a set of lockers. His talking stopped, as did everything around us. The two officers who were escorting him look stunned. My mouth was dropped as I damn near dropped.

"**Get him some help!,**" I yelled. Blood was pouring out of his head and one officer so happened to have a towel and placed it on his head. Carlos wasn't responsive and by now, the halls were packed with onlooking teachers and students. The nurse of the school came rushing in while teachers were trying to keep everyone at bay. Immediately I thought back to when I watched Fruitvale Station. I didn't see Carlos right now. I saw Oscar Grant, the same brother whose name he was screaming before he was knocked unconscious. This was all too familiar in Black America. Their book had now become my chapter, as I seen for the first time that even in the burbs, you are still a nigga in most people's eyes. They waltzed me away as the principal and medics made it to the scene. I didn't know what was about to happen to my friend. Pray was all that I could do. Here it was an hour after the incident and I was still sitting in this room. I was bored and still cuffed while sitting at this table. I swore that I felt like I was in a real episode of The First 48. All of a sudden the door creaked open. It was Mr. Lyons.

"Could you give us a minute Phil?" Phil was one of the security personnel. He walked out as I stared a hole through his body.

"Ram.....what happened?"

"**HE CALLED ME NIGGA SIR!**" Mr. Lyons just stood there. I don't know if he was more perplexed at what I told him or the way that I told him.

"Ram."

"**I'M NOT NOBODY'S NIGGA! I'M NOT HIS NIGGA! YO**

NIGGA! NOT SOME CRAB PATTY ASS NIGGA! NONE OF THAT!"

"YOU'RE A FUCKING MAN!," he yelled, slamming his hands on the table as he stared me dead in the eyes. I was immediately taken back by how angry he had just gotten. This was seeming like a bad dream. Like I was sleeping with the lights on and I finally woke up. I closed my eyes, only to re-open them to his sight. It was real. This wasn't no damn dream.

"Look here. Ramses Osiris Martin. You aint no nigga. You're a man. Tell me. If I said Pangea, what does that mean to you?" I kinda leaned back in my seat, trying to figure out what he was trying to get at.

"Sir, what does Pangea anything have to do with this?"

"Just answer my question." I stared at him for a good thirty seconds. I thought I would intimidate him, but it was to no avail.

"Enlighten me......sir."

"Gladly," he responded. What you are about to hear will be extremely disturbing. If you listen to this and can actually wrap your head around it, you will never be the same. "PANGEA." It was a time when earth was all connected as one giant supercontinent. Now I have a question. Were people living and thriving during this time? If they were, and we know they were, this means Morocco was in the New England region of the United States and Senegal was near Atlanta. Think about slavery. How many slaves would you need from Africa in a land filled with brown people already there? What If our history has been altered in such a way that if we just looked at basic maps, suppressed archeology and ancient structures, we can see that America and Africa are one? And let me apologize for the name Africa, 'cause that was a name given after it was conquered by a Greco-Roman emperor. So don't you ever join a Greek fraternity when you get to college,

156

because if they checked their true history, they wouldn't be doing the shit. But I get it, kids wanna be apart of something. Not callin' them bad people at all, but facts are facts. You'll never see a pro black man eating ice cream with the Klan. Instead of checking DNA for the motherland, ask yourself, what if some of our ancestors are from this very land? This is something that always interested me but seemed childish. Thank the creator for a child like mentality! The planet was populated before the continents split, which is why all races can be traced back to African DNA. Africans dispersed and navigated throughout the earth and became natives to whatever region or continent eventually broke off. Climate and temperature then determined the skin tone of any particular region. Some stayed dark, some got lighter to adjust to weather and sunlight. That also explains why the spiritual worship and building structures in indigenous regions around the world are so similar. The knowledge came from the mind of a similar thinking people that became separated by oceans. Explains why there is a whole portion of The Grand Canyon with hieroglyphics, artifacts and names embedded in its walls. If we look at that particular section, those places have Egyptian names." Right there, I was tired of him talking.

"Sir, no offense. But what is the point of you telling me all of this?" That's when he chuckled and sat down, looking dead at me.

"The point is....if you a nigga...then he a nigga. Think about it." He continued to look at me as I was stiffled in dead silence.

"Your parents are on the way. You are not in trouble...with me. You may hear from that brats parents, but you and Carlos are good with me."

"How is Carlos sir?"

"He's good. Nasty bump on the top of his head, but he'll

157

be okay. I'll be looking at security camera footage later, but he will be fine. You think about what I said though. I mean... think." Mr. Lyons walked out of the room. As I sat there by my lonesome, I started to think outside of the box. Why did he tell me what he just told me? What was he trying to prove? Just then, the door opened back up.

"Oh yea, one more thing," he said. "Look up the Niger Region. Research it. Then talk to me at a later date and time." I sat there until my mom came to pick me up. She talked to Mr. Lyons, but she really didn't pay attention to him. This was proven by her constant drilling of me as we drove home. I didn't understand. My mom rarely got angry. In this case however, even after explaining it to her, she still didn't wanna hear it.

"Ramses, just stay in your room," she yelled as we came through the house door.

"What's going on?," my father asked, putting his Nat Geo magazine down.

"Honey, our son got into an altercation at school. All because someone called him out of his name. You need to control your anger Ramses. **CONTROL IT!**" I looked over at my dad and he clearly had a confused look on his face.

"Son, what exactly did the student call you?"

"What you think dad? What other word do you expect these highly privileged kids to call me?"

"**THAT DOESN'T MEAN YOU LOSE IT!**" By then, I was tired of her ranting.

"**NO MOM. I AM FUCKING LOSING IT!**" Right then and there, her body literally froze.

"You think I asked for this. I didn't ask you to come get me from Oklahoma. I didn't pray to God that I hope some well off white family comes and adopts me, takes me away and have me live happily ever after. I don't relate to this shit. I never have and I never will. You know what I learned since being here? Its that I'm still black. I go to Birmingham, I ain't black enough. I play football against Crenshaw, Fairfax or some other inner city school, and I ain't one of them. I walk through the halls of school and I'm the stereotypical black male. You can't understand what that feels like mom. You think I'm their golden child. **FUCK NO!** I run a football for a thousand yards, make hundreds of tackles and everyone cheers. After the game, I'm just the black boy on campus with a few other black boys who make the team good. Or somewhat good. Ah hell, let's face it, we just a decent team. A big ass team with a few bright spots. I ain't important. Maybe a few like me, but the majority could give a damn. In their eyes, I got white parents, so it's obvious I am either an adopted, troubled child or an orphan from Africa, or some shit. No matter what mom, it ain't good enough. It ain't good enough for black folks, it ain't good enough for white folks. I'm just a shadow. Fuck it. I'm a shadow."

I turned around and walked upstairs. There was nothing more for me to say. I had gotten everything off my chest that I had been holding in for eight years. As I entered my room, all I could do was fall on my bed and stare at the ceiling. It sucked saying what I said to the woman who gave me another chance at life, but it needed to be said.

"Son, can I come in?"

"Sure dad." My father came in my room and shut the door. He stared at me, not knowing what to say for the longest.

"Ram.....I'm sorry."

"Dad, its not your fault. I'm not mad at you. I'm just a little upset because mom doesn't understand." Pops took a deep breath.

"Son...truth is. Neither one of us understands you." He came and sat next to me on my bed. "When we adopted you in Oklahoma many moons ago, all we seen was a young man who had all the potential in the world. In the last eight years, we raised that young man and I am damn proud of the man that you are becoming. At the same time, in the last eight years, we never got to know you."

"Dad....what are you talking about? You know me inside and out. You know my likes and dislikes. What are you talking about?" He looked up towards the sky as if he was silently praying to have the right words come out of his mouth.

"Ramses, formerly known as Brian Carter. I will never know what it's like to be black. I have a black son. I used to just see you as my son. But from what happened today, I realize that no matter what, you have a struggle that I will never have to deal with. I never tried to understand what it was like to be black. I never had to face it. I never had to face poverty, gunshots, drugs or racism on an astounding scale. I never did. Now, as your father, I saw you for the first time become enraged by being hated for who you are. I was so blind to the fact. Maybe your mother was too. All we seen when we adopted you was hey, we just came back from Alkebulan, what people call Africa today. Ancient Kemet. I wanna give someone a chance who may not have one is what I told myself, since someone gave me the chance to explore their beautiful country. Oh don't be fooled. Over there it's not all flies and starving kids. They would make you believe that because that is all they show. The majority of the people over there are prosperous and very, very, knowledgeable. Anywho, I've failed you. All these years I was so busy getting to know my son, that I failed to get to know my son. Please accept my apologies and help me become a better parent to you?"

We stared at each other. I God honestly didn't know what to say. There were heartfelt words and then there were heartfelt words. I never imagined hearing anything like that in my life from my dad, but it happened. There was a knock at the door. My mom opened up. With tears in her eyes, she just ran over and hugged me. I hugged her back and my father wrapped his arms around us both. Nothing else was said vocally, but these actions spoke volumes. I think we all learned a lesson in this. None of us truly understood each other. I don't even think my parents understood one another on all levels. It brought us all closer together. I couldn't change my situation. I couldn't change my life. I couldn't change the circumstances of being born with a high amount of melanin. I couldn't change the stereotypes. What I could change, however, is my mindset and how I react to everything. In this moment, I knew I grew up. Two weeks passed and everything was back to normal at school. Chris ass said not another word to me. I was pretty sure that he had learned his lesson about running his flap. Especially seeing that walking around with a mask on because of your broken nose didn't make you the prettiest guy walking. I was in P.E. class when Mr. Lyons came in. I was in the middle of squatting 405 a few times. I saw him in the mirror with another man, but I didn't think nothing much of it.

"Good set Ram."

"Thank you sir."

"Hey, I have someone hear who wants to meet you. This is strength coach Cameron Nichols...from U of O." My head whipped around so fast to him.

"U of O sir? Which one?" He got a good chuckle.

"The only one that matters son. The University of Oregon." I was shocked. I hadn't even considered them.

"I've seen your game tapes. You're more than impressive. Your fast, have keen sense of the ball, all of that. I wanna invite you up for a visit. Come check the campus out, meet some of the players, coaches, see the facilities, everything. You have one more year left in high school. You probably got a lot of schools beating down your door, but we want you at the best. Besides, Earl here told me that you like green. And last time Sparty green came to Eugene, we showed em that

Duck green was way better." Those were bold words and fighting words. In the same sense, I was awestruck. I mean, who wouldn't wanna put on the Oregon uniform? Hell, they had about six billion of em.

"Alright sir. Let me talk to my parents and Mr. Lyons here, and I'm golden."

"That's what I'm talking about," as he shook my hand.

"We'll talk later Ramses. Finish your workout." I was so crunk that I threw on an extra 50 to the bar. 455, six times and a bunch of energy inside of me.

"**WOOOOOOOOO!**," I yelled, not noticing that the whole gym class was looking at me crazy.

"**WOO, WOO, WOO,**" I kept shouting. I started dancing around like I was Ric Flair. I was simply the G Shock wearing, BMW riding, football flying, kiss stealing, wheeling dealing, son of a gun. **WOOOOOOOOOOOO!** This news couldn't have come at a better time. It was truly nearing decision time.

It was a crisp April morning. I got off the plane in Eugene and immediately began freezing my black ass off. I wasn't used to this. A Newport cold is maybe 65 degrees. It wasn't snowing, but it was 27 degrees. I could see my breath. I couldn't rock with this. If it wasn't for football related business, I would turn around and get back on the first plane smoking to L.A. Mr. Nichols and I got to his car, and just rapped about life while we made our way to the campus. I swear on everything I love, Oregon was hella different. I knew Tep had told me all about it when we were kicking it down in Alabama, but it was a whole different ball game seeing it for myself. One, it was green as all to be damned. It looked like it was more trees up here than people. Then, the rain started to come down. Tep had told me only two things are guaranteed in Oregon, and that was tree growth and rain. He was right.

"Alright, welcome." I was looking out the window when Mr.

Nichols said that. I turned my head back around and my mouth had just dropped. There it was....Autzen Stadium. The crazy thing is that the stadium itself didn't stand out to me. The big yellow O is what made me get goosebumps. I loved football and Michigan State most of all. When you thought of Oregon, however, several and I mean several big names came to mind. Ontario Smith, Maurice Morris, Lamichael James, Legarette Blount, Jairus Byrd, Patrick Chung, Haloti Ngata, Jonathan Stewart. I mean, there were some big time guys who had came through this program. Rose Bowls, National Championship appearances, God knows how many ten win seasons. It was truly a jaw dropping experience to be here.

"Are you ready," he asked me, parking dead smack near the entrance.

"Hell yea sir. Let's go." We got out the car and walked inside. Before we even hit the locker room, I was on cloud nine. I had seen colleges before, but I had never had an experience like this ever. This was my first college visit relating to sports. Once we hit the locker room, it was like walking into a different world. I seen all of the jerseys hanging up in here. I don't know if they set this up for me or what, but it was humbling to say the least. We made it through. I was completely immune to what Mr. Nichols was saying to me. I was in heaven. Then.....then.....we hit the tunnel.

"Stop right here." I did. I saw at what looked like mid field, a group of men and the duck mascot.

"Now, wait for the crowd noise to be heard over the loud speakers and run out. As a matter of fact, take off your coat and put this on." He reached into his coat and pulled out a black home jersey. It really felt real now. Ignoring the cold, I tore off everything above my waist and threw this on. I closed my eyes and imagined the first time that I ever strapped on a helmet and some shoulder pads. My first run in high school was an 86 yard touchdown run against Huntington Beach High. It was my introduction to the state of California and the world. We won that night 40-23. I was just a sophomore when it happened. 24 carries, 256 yards on the night and three touchdowns. I finished that season with 1,936 yards and 34 TD's. Last year, I added defense to my resume by starting at outside linebacker. As for offense, well, I trumped 2,000 yards and scored 43 TD's, as coach literally made me a Marshall Faulk time workhorse. I would've had more, but in our second playoff game, I was put out by a vicious hit to my knee in the second quarter. I didn't tear anything thank God, but I was out for the game. We ended up losing 34-21 and it only fueled my fire for me to come back stronger, especially seeing that we were down 28-21 with only 4:32 left to go in the game. As I opened my eyes and came back into reality, I heard the recorded crowd noise over the loud speakers in the stadium.

"It's your time Ramses. **RUN OUT!!!**" I took off into a full on sprint. In my vision, I saw a full house going crazy. Nothing but a sea of green and yellow. This experience made me wanna skip my senior year and head straight to college. I ran as if I were wearing all red and I was in a Crip neighborhood. Finally, I stopped in the middle of the field. Whoever was in the duck mascot outfit started doing pushups. I always seen this on TV at their games, but to see it in person was a whole 'nother story. Hell I felt like De'Anthony Thomas when he ran 94 yards against Kansas State in the Fiesta Bowl and I was just at midfield.

"Welcome son to the most important decision in your life," one of the gentlemen said. We rapped at midfield for a good ten minutes until one of the coaches signaled to the tunnel where Mr. Nichols was still at. I turned around to see six bruhs all walking towards me.

"Son, I want you to meet some of the greatest players in

the world. Matter of fact, they are the greatest players in the world." The closer they got, it looked like six gladiators instead of football players.

"Sup man. They call me Rambo." Everyone, including the coaches started to laugh.

"Well Rambo, take this young man with you guys and talk to him. Let him know what Oregon football is all about. I shook all of the coaches hands and walked off with the players. I got to the locker room with the players coach sent me with.

"Where you from bruh?," one of em asked.

"Newport Beach." The whole room burst out into laughter.

"Newport? Newport. Man, you living the good life." Here we go again I thought. All I could think about was being at that football camp way back yonder and those cats from Compton were ready to roll me up into a human blunt.

"A man, don't take what my mans said personal," said this huge, burly built dude. He had to be a D lineman or an O lineman of sorts.

"Look, usually, when we meet the bruhs up here, they usually from L.A., the Bay, Texas, few niggas from the East Coast, maybe Chicago, but Newport? Nah. Man I wish I had known how to deal with these white folks when I came up here."

"So where you from?" I asked him.

"Bruh I was raised in Oakland. Got a scholarship coming out of Fremont. All I seen in my life was street niggas from East Oakland. Hell, all I knew was the Bay. Moms got us out a few times. Furthest was when I went to Mississippi for a fam reunion. All I knew was street niggas and Mexicans. Then... then...then enter Oregon. Man I got up here and it looked like paradise compared to East Oakland. Niggas had trees that weren't dead and shit. Well paved roads. The air....the air was actually breathable. Everywhere I went, white folks asked do you play for the ducks? I told em yea, but I was like damn. In the back of my mind I thought is this the only time they are accustomed to seeing someone black folks. I'm not knocking the experience 'cause it has taught me a lot in three years. All I'm saying is that it was indeed an eye opener."

"Yup and I'm fucking the shit outta all this white pussy." We all laughed as that was their running back walking through the locker room talkin mess. I mean, rapping with these dudes gave me insight on more than what the university was about. It showed me what the black experience was truly like. Once my day finished up, I got back to the hotel and really researched this place. I typed in Eugene, Oregon. I know Wikipedia could be screwed up seeing how it was a public domain that people could alter at anytime. For the most part though, it gave me the information that I always needed.

"Wow," I said out loud. For a city of over 150,000, it was 1% black. That told me right there that the only people here with some dark skin were the college athletes and maybe a few professors. I had dealt with that my whole life. As much as a golden opportunity this was, I wanted something different. I hadn't been around my culture ever. The only way I was gonna get that was by going to an HBCU. Then again, there was that dilemma of wanting to play for the best sports team possible to have a shot at winning a national championship. It was a dilemma that I truly faced. I didn't wanna face it, but that's life in a nutshell. It is simply a bunch of experiences you don't wish for. You just simply endure them and hope something good comes out of it at the end. The most important thing, however, is that you learn from the decisions you make. I only had a year left of high school and where I went from there would probably be the most important decision of my life. From there, I started using the world's new version of a book called Google to see what I could come up with about this place and maybe Oregon in general. What I found was a story written by Pete Shaw entitled

"Why aren't there more black people in Oregon?" The article read as follows:

"When is history not history?" asks Walidah Imarisha, at a recent Why Aren't There More Black People in Oregon? presentation sponsored by the Oregon Humanities Conversation Project. Imarisha, a Portland State University and Oregon State University instructor, poses the question to our group after we have spent 90 minutes examining, wrestling with and, mostly importantly, discussing with one another the history of black people and black communities in Oregon. The question is imposing – forcing us to look to the past and present for answers, and demand an honest reckoning for the future. There are small posters on the walls of our conference room in the Midland Branch of the Multnomah County Library, forming a timeline of history ostensibly relating to black Oregonians. On one, there is a picture of Marcus Lopes, the first person of African descent in Oregon. Another item features Alonzo Tucker, a black man who was lynched in Coos Bay. A local newspaper described the lynch mob as "quiet and orderly" and found the lynching was not an "unnecessary disturbance of the peace." Time may move along, but progress can seem frozen in its eddies.

A law prohibiting black people from voting remained in the state constitution until 1927. A connection to the Confederacy with a law prohibiting interracial marriages, only repealed in 1951. An item about Legacy Emanuel's 1970 expansion that ripped a hole in the Albina neighborhood, after the project lay stagnant for nearly two decades resulting in vacant lots and boarded up buildings. It is still being completed. A photo of Mulugeta Seraw, the Ethiopian graduate student and father beaten to death by two skinheads in 1988. Laws, events, customs-all the stuff not just of history, but also of resistance, achievement, and ultimately, survival. In 1844, pre-state Oregon declared slavery illegal. But making slavery against the law and embracing a diverse society are two different items, and from its beginnings Oregon was modeled as a white homeland. That same 1844 law ordered all black people out of the Oregon Territory under threat of lashing. This "Lash Law" mandated black people be publicly flogged every six months; however, before it could be enforced, it was modified and the whippings were replaced with forced labor. In 1849 another law excluded any more blacks from settling in the territory. The passing of the Oregon Donation Land Act of 1850, granted free land to Whites only. The 1859 constitution included in its Bill of Rights a racial exclusion clause banning black people from emigrating to Oregon, as well as prohibiting them from owning land and entering into contracts.

Although the 14th and 15th Amendments to the United States Constitution rendered such exclusion illegal, it wasn't until the 1920s that the ban was officially repealed from Oregon's constitution. This history, hardly exhaustive, is the substrate of the state of Oregon, and yet it tends to be seldom acknowledged, and, when recognized, usually depicted as an artifact of the past. This is one point where history is not history - when events are isolated, ignored, or otherwise relegated to a sphere where that is rarely discussed and where the societal effects of that history dwell without context. When you digest and discuss all those images and descriptions on the wall - as Imarisha encourages you to do with people whom you do not know - a narrative emerges. These snapshots that unto themselves seem aberrant, the work of vile individuals or groups, such as the Ku Klux Klan, start running together, becoming a movie with obvious currents that formed with the state and flow into the present.

Measure 11, establishing mandatory minimum sentencing for several crimes, was passed 150 years after that first exclusion law. It applies to all defendants over 15 years old and require the accused of the listed crimes be tried as adults. Despite making up only 4 percent of Oregon's youth population, black youth account for 19 percent of Measure 11 indictments. It seems William Faulkner was right: the past isn't even past. But if our state story reveals some of the horrific and disgusting acts committed, laws promulgated, and customs enforced, it also depicts acts of resistance that in themselves form a narrative. Resistance is a slippery concept, for its successes may come incrementally and some seem nothing more than drops upon a toxic pool. For example, in Bend in 1925 there was a sign that read, "We Cater To White Trade Only." The black community in Bend, already aware of the local restaurants in which they were unwelcome, protested the sign.

The city council agreed to remove it and similar Jim Crow signs, with the expectation that black people would now police themselves. Though the victory may seem Pyrrhic, it was an important step for those forced to daily encounter the signs and be reminded of the ways in which they were unwanted. It took thousands of these small largely unknown victories, won by tens of thousands of people you and I will never know, that ultimately led to the Civil Rights Act of 1964. Many of the institutions that shape our lives today are rooted in the Oregon constitution, and the legacy of the exclusion clause can be seen by observing where those institutions grant favor. One of the most glaring examples lies in housing and development. For the black community in Oregon, it has often been a history of taking and denial. Since homeownership is a foundation of generational wealth development, it becomes clear that Oregon's black community is being denied an opportunity to develop wealth. The places where black people could own property were limited through extra-legal means, such as The Portland Real Estate Code of Ethics (1919), which mandated real estate agents refuse to sell to people whose race would *"be determined to lower property values in that neighborhood."* During World War II, over 13,000 black people moved to Vanport to build ships for Kaiser – a sixfold increase in the number of black people in Oregon. The Vanport flood of 1948 forced integration on Portland, as black survivors moved a couple of miles north to the Albina neighborhood, the only place the city would allow them to resettle. The 1960 construction of Memorial Coliseum resulted in the destruction of over 400 homes and many black owned businesses, and created a physical rift in the community, particularly in Jumptown, the cultural center that ran between NE Williams and King. The construction of the interstate highways destroyed over 1100 housing units in South Albina.

Banks refused mortgages to black people who tried to move outside "acceptable" boundaries, and often refused them within the red lines as well, because those loans were considered risky. More recently banks were willing to lend money in the form of subprime loans, often when people actually qualified for prime loans. These subprime loans largely targeted minority communities, and the current foreclosure crisis has hit communities of color hard. Black and Latino homeowners have been almost twice as likely as white people to lose their homes to foreclosure, a result, according to the ACLU in a recent lawsuit against Morgan Stanley, of the seemingly illegal and certainly unethical decision to encourage predatory mortgage loans to low-income African American borrowers. Despite the trauma, a black community is still extant in Portland. As Imarisha noted when one black woman stated, *"I don't feel like I live here. I survive here,"* sometimes survival is winning.

"For a black community to exist here in Portland is incredible," said Imarisha,

"because it wasn't supposed to exist at all." History is not history when some actors are denied acknowledgement of their roles at the expense of other actors who have parts that remain privileged. The importance of Why Aren't There More Black People In Oregon? is difficult to understate. It keeps the unprivileged stories alive. Though Imarisha has made this presentation all over the state, she has only met one person who attended an Oregon public school who was aware of it. None of the ten people in our group who had attended school in Oregon had been taught this information. That is when history is not history. But history is history when people refuse to let go, when they fight for their stories to be heard, and when they spread those stories. to other people who in turn pledge to keep them alive.

That is real power of this presentation. It is not a lecture. It is a series of discussions, some one-on-one, some in groups of four or five, and some with the group as a whole. Real people and their stories spoken, life breathed into the material hanging from the walls. When a woman notes how in the early 1950s the majority of restaurants in Portland would not serve black people, we see how that step taken in Bend in 1925 formed a link in a chain to today where, at the very least, such obvious segregation is unacceptable. When a man talks about how he has to pay an extra fee for his son to play in the school jazz band, it is easy enough to draw a line between the razing of four or five jazz clubs that stood in the way of the future Memorial Coliseum. Their demise meant not only fewer opportunities to experience a unique American art form, but also fewer popular culture venues where white and black people actually mixed.

Though jazz has declined in popularity to the extent that

students must pay extra for it, still it survives, vibrantly. That is a victory. Much of the physical structure of the black community in Portland has been demolished many times over. Nature took a hand in Vanport, but it was the usual systemic oppression of the wealthy and powerful that led to Memorial Coliseum, the construction of the interstate highways, and the expansion of Legacy Emanuel. The black community has rebuilt every time. These are all huge victories. Perhaps history becomes history when it expands beyond boundaries and reaches a greater audience.

The point of Why Aren't There More Black People In Oregon? is meant not to focus solely on the black community and its history, but to explore issues of race, identity, and power in the greater community. The struggles and victories of black people are not unique. As can be seen with Multnomah County Sheriff Staton's collaboration with Immigration and Customs Enforcement (ICE), Latinos are facing their own trials. The exclusion laws from the early Oregon Territory and Oregon state constitution echo loudly, as the brave people proclaiming themselves Undocumented and Unafraid speak of the terror they experienced from being identified as people who do not belong, and whose existence within the community can be severely punished. The same scenario is going on nationwide. A history that ignores uncomfortable aspects – whitewashes them, if you will – so that what is presented is a sanitized account with no accountability, is at best insular.

It does not require thought, and therefore, does not challenge. It only asks that we accept its narrative as truth. It is mythology, not history. The posters that form a timeline ostensibly related to black Oregonians actually relate to us all. They are a part of our history, informing our present and likely our future as well. How just a future we craft largely depends on how wide and deep a sense of history we bring along on the journey forward.

"When we see these events as part of a cycle," Imarisha said, "then we can see what is really happening and can create a place we want to live in." I closed my laptop, got up and looked at myself in the mirror.

"What Chapter? What Chapter?," I kept asking myself. What black was I and what black did I want to experience? My battle and struggle continued.

8 THE FINAL RIDE

Enter the car slow
keep hands on the wheel
and feet on the brakes

"Listen up gents. For many, this is your first ride. For others, this is your final ride. For the ones who have busted their ass, sweat out the pain, shed the blood and turned into complete monsters on a Friday night, this is it. Your final ride. At times, you may have hated me. At times, you may have wanted to kill me, blow up my house, strangle my dog, whatever. I'm glad you did, because it told me that I did my job. I'm not here to make star athletes. I am here to make you men. I don't care how many yards you run for. I don't care how many tackles you make while you are here. If you don't leave here being a better MAN than when you started, then I have failed you. There are a million people who can run a football or shoot a basketball. There aren't a million people, however, who can grow in that process. I once memorized a quote form the great Ray Lewis himself. He said You've got to go out and show them that I'm a different creature now then I was five minutes ago, 'cause I'm pissed off for greatness. Cause if you ain't pissed off for greatness, that just means you're okay with being mediocre. So with every minute that passes in life, you get better. With every second that passes on that field, you get more resilient. You dig deep, you claw, you scratch the back of the man whose hands can't reach and you walk the path of the man with two broke feet. You go out, lay it all on the line and you fucking win.....in life. Not the field, but life." It was so quiet that you could hear a rat piss on cotton.

"Now let's get out there and kick some ass." We erupted in a roar for the ages. Coach walked out and we got into our zone ready to go. It was senior year. Its was our time. More importantly, it was my time. As we ran out onto that field, it all of a sudden felt like being at U of O once again. It felt like it was just me out there and that I was, the one man show. I could see my future in the distance. I was so close that I could taste it. It was time to open the flood gates. We were almost at the halfway point of the season. We were 4-0 and facing our hated rivals Huntington Beach High tonight. I could careless about them as a whole, but one of them I did care for a lot.

"Sup dawg?" I shook up with Nathaniel at mid field about seven minutes before game time. Nathaniel Means was like me. He was a sprinkle of black in a majority white community. He was the star on this team. The anchor of the defense. They were 2-2 this year, but if you counted records based on his performance alone, they were undefeated. Through four games he had an astounding 64 tackles and eight sacks. Dude was a monster. He had already committed to Boise State at the end of his junior year.

"So you joining me up in Potato land mane?" I got a good chuckle from that.

"Man now you know that blue hue ain't for me. I'm thinkin green baby. Sparty or the Ducks."

"Just remember last time them Ducks came to the land, horses ran amuck, something you won't do tonight."

"Yea aight boy. Don't break no bones trying to tackle me, seeing how you too slow to catch me and to weak to take me down." We both laughed and dapped up.

"Let's make this last one a good one bruh," he said.

"All day," I responded. We jogged back to our respective sidelines and started to get ready for what was the last time we would meet each other in high school. The score was 17-13 late in the second quarter.

"44 dive, 44 dive. Ready....BREAK!!!" We broke the huddle and I stepped back to my position. I scored once already and had amassed 71 yards on 14 carries so far. All I honestly thought was that this would be another play like any other. The ball was snapped, I followed my fullback through the hole. He took on the outside linebacker, who was involved in a cross blitz. That left Nathaniel the ability to roam free. As soon as I got pass the initial line of scrimmage I seen him. In a split second, we both lowered our shoulders and the boom was heard all around the stadium.

Two yards weren't much, but it was enough for the first as we only needed one yard on third down. I got up, shaking off the sting from that hit. As I walked back to the huddle, I heard a bunch of whistles. I turned around to see Nathaniel on the ground. He was motionless. As we all took a knee, I thought nothin' of it. Nate was 6'2, 235 of sheer solid titanium wrapped up in human skin, so I knew he would be straight. As the coaches and medics started to surround him, I saw his hand and lower arm start to move up just a lil bit. I was definitely good now. Any minute, he would jump up and walk off the field. Unfortunately, that didn't happen. Whatever happened during our hit, it was vicious enough to where they threw him on a stretcher. As they lifted him up on the gurney, I saw his fingers move. I walked over to him, thinking he had one helluva concussion.

"You good," I whispered.

"He smiled, but the look in his eyes wasn't normal.

"Walk for the man who has no legs bruh." He smiled again as they wheeled him off the field. Yea, that dude definitely had a concussion. I did not get what the hell he was saying to me. He was more than delusional from our collision, but concussions can do that. I finished out the game and I finished out strong. 31 carries, 246 yards and 4 touchdowns in a 52-20 romp of our neighbor rivals. I felt like Al Bundy at Polk High when I got back to the locker room.

"Ram? I need to talk to you." That was coach callin' me. I was a little pissed seeing that I was ass naked with a towel on and about to shower. He just couldn't wait. He had to talk to me now.

"Sup coach," as I walked in his office.

"Your friend is paralyzed from the waist down." My heart stopped. I really wasn't comprehending what he had just told me.

"Coach, could you repeat that to me?"

"He's paralyzed Ram. He had a message for you at the hospital. He said it's still Boise State over everything. Just thought I'd let you know." I walked out of his office and into the training room where no one was at. I sat on the training table and just delved deep into my thoughts. I gave my all to this game. I wanted to have fun and do something that I loved. Now, I was rethinking all of this. In my pursuit of happiness, I took someone else's happiness from them. I don't know how long I sat there, but it was long enough for the janitor to come tell me that I needed to hurry up because he was ready to lock up the building. I went and threw on my sweat suit, and headed to my car. I didn't drive directly home.

I rode out to the beach. I texted my mom to let her know that I was alright and that I was sorry for not meeting with her and dad after the game. I just sat on the rocks and listened to the waves crash along the shore. This one incident had changed my life in a way I never imagined. I didn't wanna play football anymore. Worst than that, I felt like a traitor against my own. Here we were. Two young black men making it in environments that really didn't relate to us. I took one of us out.

Now....it was all over. I sat out there till about 12 o'clock that Friday night. I didn't even realize what time it was until my mom called me asking where I was. I quickly apologized for losing track of time and hauled tail home. Once I got through the doors, mom was waiting for me with a look in her eyes that said "Mother" more than "mad."

"Ramses honey, I am so sorry for your friend." She quickly wrapped her arms around me and just comforted me. I was down. I mean, way down.

"It's all my fault mom." She grabbed me by my face.

"Its not your fault. No one could've predicted that. It's a part of the risk we take everyday. When we drive to the store, we take a risk. When we walk up the steps, we take a risk. There are risks with everything in life, but you can't go through life blaming yourself for everything bad that happens when it involves you." Those words, those words right there, shook me to my core. It brought me back to a dark place. Deep down, I felt that my parents death was my fault. I felt like my uncle's death was my fault. I didn't know what to do. Even having everything that I had in life, I felt low. I waltzed off to my room and went to sleep. At least I tried to. Saturday morning came around and I saw myself arise at 6:30 A.M. I left my parents a note and went out to the beach for a jog. The morning air was crisp and clean. I threw on my elevation mask and started to run thru the sand.

I was in a whole other zone. Truthfully, I was in a whole new world. My mind was taking me places that it had never been. After running up and down the beach for about 30 minutes, I stood there drenched in sweat, looking at the sky illuminated by the sun that was mostly over the horizon. Last night hadn't escaped my mind. Every time I took a breath, it was like I was back at that play. We collided. That was it. It shouldn't have ended like that. I walked back slowly to my car, knowing what the only step in the healing process would be. That was face Nathaniel at his worst. I only hoped that he could find it in his heart to forgive me.

I arrived at the hospital a little bit after eight o'clock in the morning. I stalled for a moment and just sat in my car. I said a silent prayer hoping that I could say the right words to help him out. Finally, I got out. "Hello sir. Oh, you're that star running back for Newport. Great game last night." How she could be so ecstatic at a time like this beat me.

"Nathaniel Means room please?"

"Sure. Lets see......lets see. Room 219."

"Thank you. I'll find it." I walked off in my own zone. Following the signs and roaming the halls, I was hoping that I could see someone in worse condition than him. I know it sounded kind of messed up to say, but it was how I felt at the time. I wasn't one of those people who goes back on the words that I spoke. If I said it, then I meant it. I might feel different five or ten years from now, maybe even five or ten minutes from now. Either way, however, I stood by what I said in the moment and at that moment, whatever that may be. I got right outside of his room. I didn't go in immediately. I took a deep breath. I didn't know what I was expecting to see. I walked in and moved the curtain.

"Sup foolio," Nate said. Man I thought this dude was gonna have tubes all down his throat and sleeping. He was up, vibrant and watching Scooby Doo.

"Man what the hell bruh? I thought you was gonna be drugged up or something."

"Man please. Come sit down." I took a seat next to him and started watching Scooby Doo with him in a strange way. "Man," as he chewed a turkey sandwich.

"You ever notice how Daffney always went with Fred and Shaggy never wasn't hungry?" I looked at this dude strange. I thought the medications that they may have had him on had him high as giraffe kuda snap.

"Bruh, what the hell is in that sandwich? Where yo' mama and nem?"

"Ah man, moms left early this morning. She stayed the night up here with pops and they went back to tend to my little brothers. They'll be back sometime this afternoon." As he kept eating and laughing at Scooby Doo ever so crazy, I began to get nervous of what I was about to tell him.

"I'm sorry bruh."

"What," he said, not taking his eyes off the TV.

"I'm sorry man. It's my fault you like this." He shut the TV off with the remote.

"Man lemme tell you something. This neck brace, gown and all this shit I got on now, it ain't yo' fault. I don't know what or who told you something last night, but I ain't wanting a pity party from nobody. From what they say, I got spinal cord shock. Don't know what it is and I don't really care. All I know is that I am alive. When we collided last night, immediately, my legs were non existent. I couldn't feel em. I thought damn, I'm paralyzed. This morning, I was told that may not even be the case. However, whether it is or not, it really don't matter. Bruh lemme break this thang called life down to you. I'm 17 years old. I'm a speck in the world that many of our kind don't experience growing up. I was a God all because I played football. Man oh man, I had those white folks screaming for me. But when I started to think about it years ago, I would ask myself, would they even care if I couldn't run and hit? I used to let it eat at me, until I started to just live. And last night, I was living. I wasn't worried about how people looked at me. I wasn't worried about anything. When I'm on that green turf with yard markers, I am free. When I went down last night, silently, I thanked God. If it was my last time taking steps, at least He blessed me enough to put a lick on yo' ass. See when times don't go your way, you don't falter. I may walk again, I may not. I may play football again, I may not. You see regardless, I'm still going to Boise State. I'm still gonna be a Bronco in some form, shape or way. You don't let anything derail your dreams. Especially, if you're black. We got enough dream killers within our own race as is. Screw that. You man up and put the blame on your failures on you and no one else. I will not let you sit up here and blame yourslef for how I am. This was destiny. This was my destiny. I was suppose to blast yo' ass on that field.......WITH HONOR!"

"Yea aight, Liutenant Dan." We both let out a huge ass laugh.

"Yea man I was wondering was you gonna catch that. You get what I'm saying though bruh?" I just let out a deep breath. "Yea man. I mean...I hear you and everything."

"Are you hearing me or are you listening?"

"I mean...that's when he stopped me."

"Man listen. Don't do this shit. You think Jesus blames himself for how we act all because he gave us the choice of free will?" I couldn't even say anything.

"Exactly. So if JC aint trippin, why you?" That indeed was the six million dollar question. The answer was simple. I shouldn't be trippin. I sat there for the next two hours choppin' it up with my guy. It was nothing but fun times, even in the midst of a major storm for the both of us.

"Aight my dude. I'll holla."

"100 my nigg." We dapped up and I rolled out. I walked out

of his room and right into a scene of a mentally ill man being escorted down the hall by three male nurses. I calmly went to the wall and let them go by me. Other than the strange noises he was making, he seemed like a normal human being. It was crazy what growth would do to you. In the third grade, there was a kid who was mentally handicapped named Berton. I, like all the rest of the didn't know any better third graders, used to make fun of him. One day, during gym class, I was jogging behind him. Out of my own stupidity and ill will towards a fellow human, I tripped him up. I thought nothing major of it. I was just being a punk kid who was picking on someone else. Well, it turns out that the simple fall he took wasn't so simple at all. The next day, he came to school on crutches with his mother in toe. I thought my young ass was grass. I was called to the principal's office to meet with all of them. I lied out of my teeth and said I simply wasn't paying attention, and because I ran faster, I tried to go around him, but our feet got tangled up. For some strange reason, his mother and the principal bought it and I was scott free.

I learned my lesson that day, but karma wouldn't strike me until the 8th grade. I was on the junior high football team. With the first play of the second quarter, in our first game, I went out to the slot position. A simple five and out pattern is what I was running on this play. The ball was hiked and I took off. As I planted my right foot, I turned, but my leg didn't go with me. I felt the pop and heard the nastiest sound that had ever rang through my ear canals. I wasn't a rocket scientist, but I knew my ACL was torn. I remember being whisked away in a friend's car by his parents. The next four hours were the most painful of my life. I thought it was over. The one sport that I loved to play was taken away from me. Why? All because of simple karma.

I took out someone's knee purposely in my life and now God was repaying the favor. Truthfully, I deserved it. I had no right to take his ability to walk away. I agonized for the next 11 months with surgery and brutal therapy. With each passing day, it seemed that it got tougher rather than easier. It was more mental for me than anything. I was scared shitless to even do anything else. Then, I saw one night how the world seemed to crash down on Derrick Rose. Here was a kid, an adult I should say who put his hometown on his back. He blows one ACL. Then, his meniscus goes. His circumstances were some of the worst. He became more concerned about walking and running with his son in the future. I saw many turn against him. The same man who paid for a random funeral of a family that he didn't even know in his own city, the people still turned against him. For what, I thought. A fucking sport? He is a basketball player. He wasn't a crooked politician who put in secret ID laws so you can't even travel from state to state. He wasn't the person signing off on GMO foods that could modify the inside of your body in damaging ways. He wasn't any of that. He was simply a basketball player. Yet to a lot of the world, he was The Pope. Everyone always talks about supporting those with mental health issues, but what about those whose mental is just messed up from one situation? I mean, it took a good while for me to become confident to even run again after I got clearance from the doctors.

It amazes me how this country is. More people give hell to people who throw or shoot a ball more than the ones who sit in suits and affect your everyday lives. Role Models? If an athlete is suppose to be a role model for someone else's children, then who is the role model for theirs? Should it be the same one who criticizes them? If you ask me, a role model is the parent. Derrick Rose can't teach your son how to tie a tie. Steph Curry won't be the one who will be on the diamond throwing your kid pitches everyday of their lives. It's the parents, the folks in the community and this country is so faulty that parents are forgetting they are the ones who are supposed to be the role model, not the television. Yet every time something goes wrong, they wanna blame the television. My question is how the hell is your son or daughter's supposed to learn from someone who they see maybe three hours a day? They see you for 24 hours a day don't they? If some people only looked in the mirror, they would see where their failure lies.

I got to my car and headed back towards the house, stopping at an In and Out burger joint along the way to pick up something for my mom and dad. I never understood to this day how they could eat this nasty, trash truck juice of some food. When I got home, there was a car in the driveway that I didn't recognize. I thought nothing of it. It was probably some of my mom and dad's nerdy archaeological buddies discussing old skeletons they had found in some rocks or some crap like that. I walked in the house and shockingly seen a case worker, an officer and an elderly black woman. She had to be in the early to mid 40's range. She looked a little bit rough as if she had been through some things mentally and physically.

"Ram...can you sit down for a minute?," my father asked. I grabbed the food bag a little bit tighter as I walked over to the couch, not taking my eyes off this woman ever.

"Son, this is Mrs. Abendale over here. She is a caseworker for the county of Los Angeles. Over here, this is Officer Warren." I really was oblivious to anything my dad was saying right now. You know that feeling you get when you just know something, but you don't want to believe it? That's the feeling that I had right about now. As the case worker began to speak, I cut her off in mid sentence.

"Lady, you don't have to say who you are. I know who this is. I can see it in her eyes. So you didn't die huh? You been alive all these years and didn't even have the damn decency to come and get your son? What kind of mother is that? What you thought you were just gonna roll up here in Newport, snatch me up and take me back home to the South? Hell naw! You see these two," as I pointed to my adoptive parents. "This is my mother and father. I don't know you or that bastard who nutted in you."

"RAMSES STOP THAT LANGUAGE!?"

"FUCK THAT MOM!," as I chucked that In and Out bag halfway across the house. "YOU GONE EXPECT ME TO BE CALM WHEN A DAMN GHOST SHOWS UP ON MY FRONT DOORSTEP? SHE AIN'T TAKING LIFE FROM ME EVER AGAIN! FUCK OUTTA HERE!" I hauled ass up the stairs, steady ignoring my mother's calls to stay down there. Everyone else in the room was quiet. I knew that was her. Hell, to be quite honest, I looked just liked her. I shut my door and just plopped on the bed. I expected at any minute for my parents to come in and give me the forgiveness talk, but it didn't happen. I thought that woman would come in and try to explain herself, but it didn't happen. Instead, about 15 minutes later, a letter was slipped under my door.

"It's for you Ram," my father yelled out. I got up and looked at the envelope. I honestly didn't wanna pick it up, but at the same time, I didn't wanna stress about the unknown. I took it back to my bed and ripped it open. I began to read its contents inside.

Dear Brian................

That's all I made it too as I ripped it up and threw it in the trash. I didn't wanna know the story, history, none of that. I wasn't gonna visit the past since I had never lived in it. It was over a far as I was concerned. I stayed in my room really trying to make sense of everything. Truth be told, it hurt like hell. That was my twin. Rather, I was her twin. I couldn't even remember what my mother looked like, but when I saw her, I saw me. I was her with a mustache and shorter hair. It was an eerie sight to see. It was as if the dead had risen and walked the earth. I walked out of my room about one o'clock that Saturday afternoon. I went downstairs. No TV on, no sounds, no sight of anyone.

"Mom, dad," I yelled out. Nothing I got. Oh well, I thought. I would just make this a chill day and sit back, and enjoy some TV. As I cut it on, I immediately cut it off. Something told me to go upstairs and get the book I had gotten from Alabama. It was like God tapped me on the shoulder and told me to read. I dipped up the stairs, damn near breaking my neck from tripping on the last step. I got my book and headed back down to the couch. I scanned the pages, opening it up to a chapter called "Mirror Image." It was scary in a way seeing how I had just met the person who birthed me after over a decade. I took notice of the opening line on the page.

"A bird with broken feet can still fly with its wings."

"Well why in the hell would it wanna fly if it knew it couldn't land?," I said out loud like someone was there with me. I totally didn't get it. I read on. In it, it talked about how the mirror image reflected the opposite person we faced in our lives. How two people who are completely different are biological twins. I didn't comprehend, nor did I agree. Then, I closed the book after about another five minutes of reading it. The line *"A bird with broken legs can still fly with its wings"* was really eating at me. I started to think outside of the box. You know the thing that most people nowadays don't do because they live inside of one. Once it hit me, I realized I was the fool. For one, a bird with broken legs could fly because its wings still worked. However, it wasn't talking about a literal bird. It was talking about a human. The most important part of the bird is its wings, which allows it to function in the air.

For us, if we couldn't walk, we could still make it to our destination in life. When you can't walk, you crawl. When you can't walk, you ask for assistance. Our wings as humans were simply our will to survive. When we can't function as normal, we must come up with extraordinary ways to reach our destination.

I closed the book and ran back upstairs, looking for the letter. I searched, scrambled, all that. I ran around like a chicken with his head cut off and tore my room up until I realized that I ripped it up and threw it in the trash. I was now devastated and on my knees going through the trash can, taking out the pieces and somehow trying to put them back together. Ironically, I had ripped up the piece of paper beyond belief except for the portion that read "Dear Brian." I was pissed at myself. I let anger control me. I thought I had learned to not let things get put against me with the basketball game against Tep back in Alabama, but I obviously forgot that lesson. I let the anger of a woman whose story I didn't know get the best of me. Just then, I heard my parents come in the house.

"Mom, Dad!," I yelled as I came running out of the room. They followed me with their eyes as I raced down the stairs.

"Where is she?" They looked at each other. No answer.

"Mom, Dad Where is she?" Dad walked over to me slowly and put his hand on my shoulder.

"She's going back to die."

"Whatchu mean?"

"Hun? Give us a second will ya?" Mom walked out of the room, looking at me, followed by dropping her head down in the process.

"Son, as you can tell, your birth mother isn't dead. That ain't rocket science cause hell you just seen her. What you didn't know was that months ago, she contacted us out of the blue. She was diagnosed with a rare kidney disease called

Autosomal dominant interstitial kidney disease. Just know that she can't find a transplant patient and it's to the point of taking her life." I looked at my dad in disbelief. If there was a feeling of being lower than shit, then that was the way I was feeling right now. All I could do was look at him. No words were coming out of my mouth as I couldn't muster up the strength to say anything.

"Well son? Do you have anything to say about this?"

"I'm wrong dad. I...I..I can't even look at myself in the mirror right now."

"Son," as he placed his hand upon my shoulder. "If your reflection changes, then be ashamed. If it doesn't you learn from it." He walked out the room and left me there to ponder in my thoughts. I sat on the edge of my bed, upset at myself. In less than a two day span, I saw myself take out a good friend of mines forever on the football field and basically shit on my birth mother. It showed me the power of a story. How not to judge a book by its cover. Words are written to manifest and bring life to pages. And right now, the story that I needed chapters written about remained blank. All because of my inability to wanna read and understand.

I didn't do much for the next couple of hours but sit in my room. My phone rang with friends calling, but I just ignored them. As three o'clock rolled around and I still found myself lying in the bed, face up towards the ceiling, I caught a glimpse of the picture on my wall. I got up and walked over to it, analyzing it and reading the golden plate below it. Ramses Martin, First Team All State. I looked down and lifted up my right sweat pants leg. I looked at the almost three inch scar on my right knee. The 17 clips and two titanium screws that were inside told a story that I would never forget. I took off my shirt and walked over to the mirror.

"Christ servant till my death and beyond," with Psalm 34 underneath it was the only tattoo that my parents would allow me to get while under their roof. The only reason they allowed me to get that is because of my outstanding season in 2013. What a magnificent year that was. As a sophomore and the number two running back, I amassed 1,287 yards on 267 carries. I scored 15 touchdowns that year on the way to the school's first all state selection in a long time. It was really my introduction to the world. I started to smile thinkin' about the old times. I had sense enough, however, to know that living off your accomplishments in the past means nothing. I had more pressing times occurring right now and I needed to get my focus back and fix who I was as an individual. It was time to leave Ramses Osiris Martin for a moment and go back to being Brian Carter III, even if for a lil bit.

"Hello."

"Fred. Family. I need you."

"What's cracking?"

"I need to know everything. I need to know who my mama really was." The noise on the other end of the phone got silent. It was a long and concerning pause, and I knew that I had struck a chord with him.

"Fred...talk to me." A sigh let out on his end.

"Your mama wasn't always the woman she was. Your daddy made her that way." The story went as follows. Moms and pops had known each other since grade school. He was the cool, swaggerific dude who had more charm than Lucky himself. Fred explained that ever since they were little, pops had a thing for the ladies.

"He could talk a guppy into eating a shark," Fred said. "He was that type of nigga." Moms, on the other hand, well she was raised in the church. I mean, she was strictly in the church. Her parents didn't let her travel to far from the house, not even when she entered her high school years. Pops was a year older than her, but they were in the same grade. One day, during their senior year in high school, pops came over to her crib when both of her parents were working nights.

"That's the night he took her virginity and the night they actually both fell in love."

"Wait, wait, hold on. You say my pops was a slick talkin gigolo, so how in the good hell did he fall in love with her?" With a loud ass laugh, Fred told me straight up.

"After they finished and she had calmed down from the trauma as she called it, she pulled out all of his clippings from basketball season. I'm talkin bout all four years of basketball season. In all his time, he had never seen someone care that much about him, not even his own parents. After high school, they both ended up going off to college. They both ended up at Western Alabama. It wasn't a D1 school or a major powerhouse that you heard about all day every day, but it was a chance for him to get an education. At the beginning of his junior year, he was prepped for a big season. He had won conference player of the year and made Division II All American the previous season. Averaging 24 points and seven dimes a game, the team had the highest confidence that they could make a deep run in the tournament. Then, in the fifth game of the season, it happened. He went in for an easy deuce, but he came down on the foot of the opponent, ripping his knee up easily. He tore everything, and it required 17 clips and two screws just to get him stabilized again." Right then and there, time froze for me. I immediately looked down at the scar on my knee. Me and dad were more similar than I could ever imagine. It was then that his life spiraled out of control. He ended up finishing school, but the last two years he got through it by delivering "the goods" from one destination to another. My mother hated it, but she loved him so much that she stuck with him. Upon graduation, she was five months pregnant with me and they both saw no other way to put food on the table than to keep doing what they had known for the last two years. It worked, all up until that fateful night. But then Fred changed his tone.

"Your mother didn't die like you previously had thought. I apologize for keeping that hidden from you. When the car was over on its side and they were shot up, for the love of God she survived. As they were heading to get the gas can, she crawled out of the busted window and into the heavy brush on the side of the road. Everything was so dark that they didn't even see her escape out of the car. They just poured gas, lit the match or whatever and there it was. The car went up in flames. I wouldn't know on the status of your mom until a year and a half later, when I got a random phone call. She was so devastated by everything and the fact of losing you that she didn't wanna return to Oklahoma and look for you, seeing that you thought mommy was dead. She never told me what happened after the fools left, or how she made it to a hospital. That will remain a secret in her head until she is in the grave. All I know is that she is still alive and out there somewhere." I paused for a good minute before I spoke my next words.

"She made it here. To Newport Beach."

"**WHAT!!!**" Fred screamed that out as if someone had taken all his money.

"**WHAT THE HELL YOU MEAN?!**"

"She was here Famo," as I cried tears.

"I knew who she was, but I shunned her away, all because of my spite." All I could do was cry. I couldn't contain it and I hurt myself more than anything.

"Look.....look.....look...hey....stop crying man. Let me talk to you." I started to calm down and come back to my senses somewhat.

"It's alright. You were hurt. It's normal. But now that you know, just pray man. Just pray you get that chance again. If not, then all you can do is be a man and learn from it. We all mess up in life. The same way I enhanced you to pull a trigger when you were down here. I did that for me so my hands wouldn't have blood on them and I feel bad every day. I loved your dad so much that I felt the proper way to get some payback was to have his seed do it. When in truth, it should have never happened. I tried so hard to make you into what I thought was black, that I failed to realize you were never less black than me or the next man. Your book was never wrong. I was reading the right chapter. I was just too stupid to understand what was written in front of me. I'm sorry." Hearing that gave me a new sense of life. It was only one thing I could say at that point.

"Keep reading Fred, cause my story is still being written." Next Friday was here and it was game time. My mind had been heavy all week with the events that had occurred. I had to put everything behind me as we were playing Antioch. ESPN put us on as a nationally televised high school game of the week. We were both undefeated and primed to make runs in our respective CIF divisions. This really had been the longest road trip I had ever been on. We were up here in the BAY. The yay area. E-40, Too Short, Mac Dre and many more legends were from up this way. We were playing in the Oakland Coliseum, so it made the game even more intriguing.

"How you feel being home?," I asked Carlos, strapping up his cleats.

"I dunno bruh. I dunno. You ever felt like you were a prime target because you made it when it wasn't necessarily your call?"

"So you tellin me you still wanna be stuck here?"

"Naw nigga naw. It ain't that. But I mobbed these streets for fifteen years. East Oakland man. Do you know what it's like in East Oakland? You know the history of East Oakland? You just don't leave this place and become a different nigga. I dunno man. I'm still the same. I'm just nervous that some of the homies won't think that way." As he continued to get his gear together, I tried to enter his mind. I wondered how it would be if I went back to Oklahoma with the same kids I was in foster care with? I God honestly didn't know where any of them were at, but how would they feel about me? What if they seen me now and they were still stuck in the system? Would I be the brother they knew for two years or would I be a foreigner? I tried to understand his walk, but I wasn't in his shoes, so it was very, very difficult. **TOUCHDOWN ANTIOCH!!** They scored twice in seven minutes as we were now down 14-0 with less than five left in the first quarter.

"GET YOUR SHIT TOGETHER!!! FUMBLE THE NEXT ONE RAM AND YOUR ASS WILL BE PARKED HERE WITH ME FOR THE REST OF THE NIGHT!" Coach was chewing out the offense, but particularly me because I just coughed up the ball and watched them scamper 67 yards for the score. We were clearly overmatched. Carlos was flaring up, the whole team was pissed and it looked like we weren't gonna gain any momentum. I glanced over to their sidelines to see one of their coaches, Josh Bulla, jumping up and down in excitement as his team was running on all cylinders right now. I had heard about this guy. He was an ex military man who was a beast on the football field. He was an all everything receiver and quarterback playing for the service in Guam and at Camp Pendleton, CA. Right then and there, I knew everything was on me. The next kickoff came and I was primed.

"Kneel Ram kneel." I wasn't hearing Kevin talking to me. I caught that bitch six yards deep in the end zone and ran like it was no tomorrow. I skipped, jumped and stiff armed anything that was in my way, to include my own teammates. I was in my own zone. It was like running out of the tunnel at Oregon again. I saw no one but myself, the crowd and the crazy duck mascot of theirs. I didn't even realize I had scored until I caught the roar erupting throughout the stadium. **TOUCHDOWN NEWPORT HARBOR!!!** Game was 14-7 with the extra point and our swagger was on 250. We were back in this thing and had all the momentum in the world. Unfortunately, that was the first and only gasp for us as for the next three quarters; we had our asses stomped into the ground. 62-31 was the final score. I had another 100 plus yard game with two touchdowns, but without a W it meant nothing.

Carlos had our other score, but his homecoming was beyond ruined. We allowed two backs to go over 150, and one of their receivers who was headed to Stanford next year had nine catches for 234 yards and four touchdowns, including three over 50 yards. We limped back to the locker room that night, all embarrassed that we squandered our shot with the national spotlight on us. Ain't no way in hell ESPN was gonna call us back. As we rode the bus on the way back to the hotel, you could hear a cricket ten miles away. We were dejected. 5-1 was still good, but any loss like that showed that much more work had to be done. I honestly just wanted to go to sleep and enjoy the flight back to L.A. in the morning. We pulled up to the hotel, anxiously awaiting a post game meal in the hotel restaurant that was privately held open for us. As always, me and Carlos were the last two off of the bus, seeing how we always sat on the back of the bus during road trips and talked.

"Good game Ram," as coach patted me on the back like he did all of us after a game.

"Good game Carlos." As we walked off I was about two steps ahead of Carlos. I got to the door.

"A traitor ass nigga." I turned around and seen the gun. Life and everything stopped right there. Immediately my thoughts went back to being in the car yelling for my dad as gas was being poured on him.

"Dad!," I screamed. In that instance, he made eye contact with me. Then, I seen nothing but flames. *POP! POP! POP! POP! POP!* The gunfire was sickening as I just dove towards the big ass plant near the entrance.

"CARLOS!!! CARLOS!!!" Coached had him in his arms, yelling his name. I ran over to my dude, telling him to stay with me.

"LOS!! LOS!!!" I don't know where the shooter ran off too and I didn't care. I was trying to keep my boy alive.

"GET HELP!!!," coach yelled. It was an agonizing scene as I kept my hands on his face, ensuring that he kept eye contact on me. Parents, staff and it seemed like the whole damn cavalry was here.

"Stay here man," I told him, as he coughed up even more blood amidst the commotion.

"LOS!!!" Just then, he looked dead at me and cracked a small smile that saw his gold's gleam with a stain of red.

"I-I-I knew it. Oakland don't love me no more." Those were the last words he whispered as he coughed three last times and went lifeless.

"CARLOS!!!," I repeatedly yelled. The ambulance made it there in about six minutes, but it was no point of even putting him on the stretcher. He was gone. I knew it. My blood soaked body stood in a trance as I watched him get whisked away for his last ride. Right then and there, my whole entire world turned black. Not black in the sense of nothing is there. I mean black...as if he turned into the black that the hood wasn't supposed to never see. Right Book, Wrong Chapter, Right? Well...explain to me how this chapter of betterment is wrong?

THE BLACK EXPERIENCE

They asked me what's the definition of my tattoos, all sixteen of em, I told em inked up poetry defining my life story, see definition is nothing more than repetition, but in repetition something always ends up missing like, what's the answer to the equation of not understanding times not caring, its separation, in the 30's it was the Jews, in the 40's it was the Japanese, in the 2000 and tens, head rags are the new form of du rags, terrorist is their new form of the word nigger, long beards and cotton garbs are the new baggy jeans and dreads, welcome my Muslim brothers to the black experience, going strong since the days of Constitutional signings, here my brothers, have a seat at the table to witness when they said all men are created equal, that we weren't a part of the equation, we were x or y, that variable that had to be figured out, but now I'm X'd out on a daily and I simply ask Y, why didn't I run from those sixteen plus shots that Laquan McDonald got close to the same East Chicago blocks I grew up on, why am I not believed when I holla out that I can't breathe, why am I gunned down for walking to my daddy's house with a skittles and a green tea, and I can't even avoid the gunshot blast when I'm pumping my own gas, that's why I'm moving to Oregon, to have somebody else do it for me, I'm traumatized, like for real, I'm so traumatized that I became a vegetarian after watching Fruitvale station, see this is what my experience is like, I am the butterfly Kendrick was talking about but most of mines are still treated like caterpillars on a hoe stroll, history repeats itself by placing one race on the shelf while the other is taken down for misuse, and to think, I used to complain about abuse, until I realized that getting hit in the chest with a phone by your moms is a helluva lot better than getting hit with a baton and slammed on the hood of the police car, and I still have that mental scar, I remember every detail of that night in Seattle, the place they call the emerald city, I was born a Leo, and I tried to be the lion and find some courage, but I couldn't do it, then I became the scarecrow, trying to think my way out of the situation, but I realized my brain was nonexistent at the time, then I became the tin man, I wanted to get some heart to fight back, but I had none, then I remembered I was in OZ, and the only OZ I knew of coming up was the prison show on HBO, so they been setting us up to get ready for a life behind bars from when we were barred in our mother's womb, so I write and spit these bars before they bar me behind internment camps with 2Chainz around my ankles, so forgive me Tauheed Epps if I don't bump your music anymore, I just don't wanna remind myself that slavery is coming back, and as a matter of fact it never left, it was transformed into the have and have not's, the wealthy and everyone else, see when they find out they can't control your mind they turn to your pockets, cause man worships money without failing to realize everyone on paper and coins is dead, so which side will you choose, tails, where you lay on your back and they rape you, or heads, where they cut it off from the rest of the body and control you, as for me, I'll stay broke, the same state my people have been in since time evolved.

9 DRAFT DAY

"Mom, Mom? Can you not make it so tight?"

"I just want to make sure you look good when you go out there in front of everyone."

"Oh dandelion. Leave the boy be. He can adjust his tie."

"Thank you dad." I loved my mom but I swore she had too much love in her system at times. I still had a full thirty minutes before I was headed into the gym to announce where I was gonna go play ball at for the next four years. The time was nerve wrecking and deep down inside of my soul, I was more nervous than a brother waiting for his HIV results, knowing that if he had it, he couldn't cure that government made disease.

"Can I be alone for a few minutes? Mom, Dad?"

"Sure son. C'mon Dandelion." Dad grabbed mom as she was steady spewing out tears of happiness. This was her big moment for me. The door shut as I just slow bopped around the locker room, pacing back and forth slowly. So much had happened in what seemed like so little time. I went over to the locker Carlos used when he was on the hoop squad for the school. The only brother on the team, droppin' mad points a game. Man my dawg knew he was athletic and gifted. That gold grill of his, I could just see it blingin in the the stands when I would watch him excite a room full of white folks with one of his acrobatic dunks. Now, all that was a distant memory, as my dawg was long gone from this earth. I sat in his locker thinkin' about how I learned so much from him. How from the moment we met each other we linked up as if we had known each other our whole lives. It was crazy not having him here right now saying some wild stuff. But the boy was a Black Panther at heart. Oakland was all through his blood, even when he was down here. Nothing can take the hood out of a man, ever. No matter where he goes.

"YOLKED ON HIS ASS!!!" That was me screaming in the stands watching Los just throw down a monster dunk on a 6'11 center from Thousand Oaks. Our section of the gym was going crazy. Los had just put us up six with 1:36 to go. Score was 67–61. Our school wasn't really known for basketball, let alone football, but the boy made it seem like we were a national powerhouse with his play. Timeout was called. Oaks just couldn't stop him this night. He averaged 31 on the year. Tonight, he had 58, meaning the rest of the team dropped nine. He wasn't a gunner or anything like that. He was just having that night where he was in a zone and he wasn't coming out of it. Oaks came out of the timeout in desperation mode. They had to do something major on defense. Even if they hit a three, with the way Los was playing tonight, he was droppin' the bottom of the net.

The inbounds came into the guard from Oaks. Here was another brother, a rarity in this school as well. Especially seeing that it wasn't a lot of black folks that I knew that could afford $25,000 tuition per year. He kept everything calm as 'Los locked in on him. He made his move. Cross left, cross right. Steal. 'Los took off with this 6'4 guard trailing him. He wasn't gonna catch him and 'Los took off in the air. Everything went in slow motion then. I was so locked in on my boy doing his thing that I didn't even notice the fat, greasy white dude come out onto the court. He pushed my mans out of the air. As I fought my way down the bleachers, I saw something that amazed me. The 6'4 guard from Oaks who was trailing ran with all he had and decked dude with a punch that came straight from hell. I was now on the court as a grip of people were over where the incident happened. Through all my emotion and anxiousness, I saw a sight that was rare in this day. I saw every black student, whether from Newport Harbor or Thousands Oaks throwing haymakers at ol' boy or anyone who was trying to stop them. Even with being rich, to most of the country, we are still niggers. All this money in the world will never matter. It looked like a rush to buy the last few pairs of J's over here.

"Hey kid," as I was snatched. I turned around and cold clocked his ass. I didn't know who he was and really didn't care. Right now, if you weren't of a dark melanin tone, you were gonna get it.

"PLEASE PEOPLE DO NOT ENTER THE COURT!" I heard the PA announcer over all of this, but it wasn't doing any good. Then........the police arrived in full force. Much like roaches when the lights cut off, we scattered. They took whoever they could catch, but they damn sure didn't catch me. It was too many kids on the court for them to just go after the black students, so they focused on just clearing everyone out. I was concerned about Carlos. I didn't see him in the scuffle. I made it out to the parking lot and scrambled to a far corner of it, full of trees, seeing how no one was focused on this direction. There was too much commotion elsewhere. I stayed there until I heard close to nothing but absolute silence and saw that the whole lot was damn near empty. No cop cars, no buses, no people at all. I had lost track of time. When I looked down at my watch, I saw that it was 10:45. I made a dash back to my car as if I were still being hunted down. I got in and peeled off, not stopping until I got to Carlos house back in Newport. I walked up the marble clad stairs of this monstrosity of a home. It was well past 12 o'clock at night and I knew his parents would be raising hell seeing me arrive at such a late hour. I rang the doorbell. The living room lights came on. I prepped myself. See, I don't know about everyone else, but when you black and you show up to a house unannounced, one or two things are gonna happen. One, you won't be acknowledged and your ass will be left standing there, getting acquainted with the door. Two, you might meet a pistol. The door creaked open to the sight of his mom in a robe.

"Ma'am. I am so sorry."

"It's okay Ramses. He said you would probably be over here to check on him. C'mon in." I walked in and shut the door.

"STINK BUTT!!! GET YA ASS DOWN HERE!!! RAMSES WAITING FOR YOU!!! You want something to drink baby?" I was stunned out my muthafuckin mind. Talk about hood.

"Uh...no ma'am."

"Stop callin' me ma'am boy. You know to call me Mrs. Tucker. Saying Ma'am make me feel old and I know damn sure I ain't. Y'all keep it down down here." As Carlos came down and she went up, she told him one last thing. "You got an hour and some change. Have em out by 1:30." Yep, this was a black mama we were dealing with.

"Sup nigga," he said as he dapped me up.

"Bruh. Nigga. Stinkbutt?"

"Man look. A nigga can't help that he shitted a lot as a baby."

"How you feeling man?" I asked him, keeping my laughter

to a low tone not to wake his folks up.

"Man when I hit the floor, I ain't even know what had hit me. All I knew was that I hit my head hard as hell and then I heard commotion. I kept hearin' mofos yell nigga this and nigga this. At the same time, I heard nigger this and nigger that. I knew it was on some ol' fuck shit. Black dude making their 'boys' look like fools. So one of them had to take it there."

"You aight though?"

"Yea. A lil cut over my right eye and a slight headache, but a nigga good. Where was you at when it went down?"

"When I saw it bruh, I just ran towards you. I hit some dude I don't even know. Its crazy cause all the black students seemed to come together. Black Lives Matter." He looked at me crazy.

"That's our problem man."

"What?," I asked him.

"Niggas hollin' that shit out now like it's the thing to do. Remember when Oscar got murked by that pig ass nigga in Oakland years back? We ran up in the police station fighting police. They ain't wanna blast that on the media though because any sign of us whoopin ass ain't conducive to the worldwide agenda. All they wanna show us doing is marching and picketing signs. You got these niggas who protesting and shit, hollin' our lives matter. They boycott Black Friday and the day before Christmas. But what about the other 30 or so days between then? Not a damn thing. See niggas love to do shit when it's convenient for 'em. Huey wasn't a one day wonder. The Panthers weren't a one day wonder. Hell nigga, they talk about Marshawn Lynch and the fact that he don't wanna speak to the media except with one word answers. But at least he consistent. These niggas ain't consistent. Jeff Fort even told the police there will be no violence without violence. And you wonder why they scared to try shit in Chicago? Plus, tell me what marching done for us, Huh? Took our communities away. How come when you go to a major joint, you never hear of an area called black town? But you can find a Jew Town, China town, Greek Town, Little Italy or any other race town for that matter except for us. Our side of the town is the hood. No neighbor in front. Just hood. You know why we say hood? Because we don't look out for our neighbors. We ain't neighbors. We ain't there. So with that aspect gone, it's just a hood. Every man for themselves. And they wonder why we can't have shit. So while all the black kids fighting together today was cool, what if that never happened? Did you attempt to talk to any of them niggas before the game? Huh, tell me? I had a long pause.

"No."

"Aight then. You didn't. They didn't. They ain't give a fuck and neither did the ones on our side. I said whats up to two of the brothers on their side as I stretched out. They gave me the you don't belong with us look. Ignored the fuck outta me. My golds and dreads were too black for em. That's the silver spoon doing that too 'em. Being raised up around Bentleys and shit, and just plain being spoiled. You different, but for most, it ain't like that. They have adapted and become like what's around them. So you saying we came together tonight? I beg to differ. You know a tape coming out. It happened at a white school and one thing them niggas got is cameras. I bet you gone be the only one on it swingin'. The rest of them was in there trying to separate it. Probably everyone except Jermaine."

"Who's that?," I asked.

"Jermaine. Jermaine Hollins. Mr. #34 recruit in the nation. Mr. I'm taking my talents to Arizona after my senior year is up. Nigga he just like me. Nigga was from Memphis. Nigga was GD to the core. I ain't even know bout them niggas 'til I met him at summer camp sophomore year. Both his parents were druggies, yet somehow he managed to balance gangbangin' and hoopin'. Finally, he got in trouble in the 8th grade for stealing. The judge was about to send him to prison, but his uncle, a wealthy former DA out here, was a connect. He brought him out here and the rest is history. Nigga got away from his environment, but it stayed in him. He learned how to control it. Now, he a B average student with uncanny hoop skills out of this world. He still a hood nigga. But he's a smart one. Why? Because now he knows both sides of the game. He knows the street game and the corporate game.

Out there, it's nothing but rich folks everywhere. His unc and his cronies gave him the tools on how to pick apart corporate America. He is now the most feared man on the planet. Because there is nothing scarier to wealthy white man than a black man with a wealth of corporate and street knowledge, who knows how to utilize it. See what you need to learn is that all your skin ain't with you. Just cause it's black don't mean it got yo back. If niggas in the hood hate each other, what makes you think the rich black nigga gone like you if you don't look like he does?"

I soaked in his words. This had turned from a session to find out how he was holding up to a full blown history lesson. I felt like I was talking to a /G\, but I wasn't. I was talking to a seventeen year old brother who had seen both sides of the game. I needed to up my game at the same time.

That memory played back in my mind as the time drew down for me to walk out and make my announcement.

"I love you bruh. Always. This for us," I whispered. Somehow, it felt like he was in the room listening to me speak. I was expecting him to come out at any minute and say shut yo crying ass up. It wasn't happening though. But I knew that he would forever live through me. I'd never let his memory die. Not as long as I had a breath in my body.

"Ramses. Are you ready?" I looked up to see my coach peeking in through the door.

"I'm bout ready as I'm ever gonna be sir." As I walked towards the door, he shut it and stopped me.

"One last time before you go. You're not gonna make me wait for the decision right.?" I just laughed.

"Coach, you know where I'm going." He smiled.

"Good luck with Sparty." He put his arm around me and walked out. Amid the sea of flashing bulbs, and numerous students and staff, I thought this was a Hollywood movie instead of a national day of commitment. As I made it to the podium, I looked down at my parents sitting there. I cracked a smile and began my speech.

"Good morning all. I thank you for coming out to my announcement for where I will spend the next four years of my life at. My life...my life....my life is not of the average kids. See my parents passed when I was four back in Oklahoma, only to find out that my mother was still alive later down the road. I hope God continues to look out for her. Followed by what I thought was both of their deaths, I spent the next few years with an uncle of mines, until he had a drug overdose and passed in front of me. I then became a product of the state of Oklahoma, spending the next two years of my life in foster care. Then, one day, two angels came in and saved me. I call them Mom and Dad. Mr. and Mrs. Martin. I was born Brian Carter III. They renamed me Ramses Osiris Martin, after the great Kings of Egypt. I arrived in Newport Beach, a black speck in an all white world. I never showed fear, never showed signs of weakness. I simply adapted to my surroundings, my new life and I made the best of it. I began to play football in junior high and I found out that I was good at it. I ran the rock for Newport Harbor for four years, amassing almost ten thousand yards total receiving and rushing. I became an ESPN top 150 recruit and became touted as the #17 rated running back in the nation. Now, this chapter of my life is over and I am prepared to move on to the next. My first game I ever seen on TV was Michigan State vs. Ohio state. I liked the color green, so they became my favorite team. And they have remained my favorite team till this day. So without any further ado, next year, I will be taking.......my talents......to the University of Wyoming."

The room was shell shocked. I saw coach spit his drink out across the room. Mr. Lyons had big eyes and couldn't believe what he was hearing. Reporters, sports writers, everyone was stunned. Folks were so banked on me going to Michigan State, but I flipped it on them.

"Oh yea, one more thing people, if I may add. C'mon out guys." Just then, eight other's came out with me. "This here to my right is Corey Wallace, #4 rated wide receiver in the nation out of Corona Del Mar. To my left, also out of Corona Del Mar is Robert Dillon, the #2 rated QB in the nation. To the right of him, is Joe Thomas, #13 ranked CB in the nation out of Mission Viejo. Down in front from left to right, we have Michael Carter, the #9 rated CB in the nation out of Lincoln High in San Diego. Also out of San Diego, from Morse High, Ronald P. Clark, #33 ranked safety in the nation. Next is Big Josiah "Flex" Perkins, #1 ranked offensive guard out of Century in Santa Ana. Next we have Darcell Byrd, # 10 ranked defensive tackle in the nation out of Dominguez in Compton. And last but not least, my close friend from Huntington Beach, the beast, the freak, the eighth wonder of the world, the #6 rated middle linebacker in the nation, Nathaniel Means." Seeing my guy walk again without assistance brought so much joy to my soul.

"They say a cat has nine lives. Well, in this world, the black man has one life. Some of us are from some affluent areas where we had to struggle with not being around our own kind. Others of us are from areas where they had to duck and dodge bullets every day. Either way, we all had to struggle in some shape or form. More importantly, we're all young black men looking to take the next step. This is now known as the black nine. Nine young brothers who came together at camp last summer and promised to have each other's back whenever, wherever. Remember, as a unit, we are one. The same way the human body is one with all 78 of its organs. Thank you." We walked off stage to the media screaming at us, trying to get answers about how we came up with our decision. I didn't even look at my parents as we scurried back to the locker room. Truthfully, my dad knew, but no one else did. As we clowned around, Mr. Lyons and coach came in the locker room.

"First off guys, congratulations. All I wanna know is this Ram. I thought you were hell bent on Michigan State?" Right then, I looked Mr. Lyons dead in his eyes.

"Sir, do you remember that bus ride after we got our asses handed to us by Antioch?"

"I wasn't on there, but I could probably guess you guys were dejected."

"Well sir, we were. As I talked to Carlos that night in the back of the bus, he said he was done with football after this. He said he wanted to focus on basketball and that he was committing to Wyoming after we graduated. For the longest he was debating whether he wanted to go to college, but he finally made up his mind. So I hit up all my partnas that I went to camp with after he died, pleading and begging them to come with me, so that we could fulfill a legacy. Carlos never asked for pity, nor for any favors. Truth is, most of these guys were going somewhere else, but the impact Carlos had on 'em at camp, it made 'em change their minds. We are the black nine sir. Just like the number nine Carlos wore in football and in basketball. Just like the nine touchdowns he had before he was murdered in cold blood. Let me ask you sir. Have you ever heard of The Ennead?" With a stunned look on his face, he responded,

"No."

"Research it sir. For as much as you have taught me, my parents taught me a whole lot more. These nine individuals you see here, we are more than human. We are a part of a bigger purpose. Sir." He scratched his head.

"Will do Ramses. You gentlemen take care." As Mr. Lyons began to walk out, he turned around immediately.

"But why Wyoming, really? Like...the real reason."

"Unfinished business," I said. "Look up the year 1969 sir." That's when he smiled at me.

"I see Carlos was more than just a bright young man. He was a revolutionary as well. Just do me a favor. Wyoming has never gotten recruits on this level ever. Don't be football players. Be great men. Make those 14 men proud."

"How did you know about the Wyoming 14 sir?"

"I never told you I didn't. You assumed I didn't."

"Rush Hour sir?"

"Just like the favorite movie of Carlos." We both cracked a smile as he turned off and walked out the room. Big Darcell then turned around to face me.

"Man what the hell was you talkin bout to that man?"

"It's complicated bruh. Trust, just know you are a part of something special."

"Nigga look. I'm a nigga from round the way. You gone have to talk to me normally my nigga." We all burst into laughter as we chopped it up for a lil bit more before we headed off to get something to eat. I got home that night around seven o'clock. There was no media, no cameras, no anything to distract me. I was a high school teenager again, if even just for a short amount of time. I went up to my parents office, seeing how they went out on a date night and scrolled the bookshelf, looking for a particular book. Finally, I found it.

"The Invisible Man" by Ralph Ellison. I had heard so much about this book when studying the great authors of the world. However, I was never able to get my hands on it. I finally saw it one day on my parents bookshelf while scanning books at random. Now, it was time to indulge. Like always, and probably the reason I ruin a good story, I always flip to some random part of a book and begin to read. As I did the same with this one, I stumbled across a part which made me feel like he wrote this about the time I was in right now.

"Women? *** damn, man! Is that equality? Is that the black man's freedom? A pat on the back and a piece of cunt without no passion? Maggots! They buy you that blasted cheap, man? What they do to my people! Where is your brains? These women dregs, mahn! They bilge water! You know the high-class white man hates the black man, that's simple. So now he use the dregs and want you black young men to do his dirty work. They betray you and you betray the black people. They tricking you, man. Let them fight among themselves. Let 'em kill off one another. We organize --organization is good -- but we organize black. BLACK! To hell with that son of a bitch! He take one them strumpets and tell the black man his freedom lie between her skinny legs -- while that son of a gun, he take all the power and the capital and don't leave the black man nothing. The good white women he tell the black man is a rapist and keep them locked up and ignorant while he makes the black mahn a race of bastards."When the black mahn going to tire of this

childish perfidy? He got you so you don't trust your black intelligence? You young, don't play yourself cheap, mahn. Don't deny yourself! It took a billion gallons of black blood to make you. Recognize yourself inside and you wan the kings among men!

Amahn knows he's a man when he got nothing, when he's naked -- nobody have to tell him that. You six foot tall, mahn. You young and intelligent. You black and beautiful -- don't let 'em tell you different! You wasn't them things you be dead, mahn. Dead! I'd have killed you, mahn. Ras the Exhorter raised up his knife and tried to do it, but he could not do it. Why don't you do it? I ask myself. I will do it now, I say; but something tell me, 'No, no! You might be killing your black king!' And I say, yas, yas! So I accept your humiliating action. Ras recognized your black possibilities, mahn. Ras would not sacrifice his black brother to the white enslaver. Instead he cry. Ras is a man -- no white man have to tell him that -- and Ras cry. So why don't you recognize your black duty, man, and come join us?

You never judge a book by its cover, just like you never judge a human by their skin color. However, I turned back to the front cover of the book just so I could play judge and jury. It really looked awkward with hidden messages hidden inside of it. I first noticed the two white lines that looked like they formed an upside down cross. I was wondering was he symbolizing his disdain for God, how we worshipped the same God that the slave master used to control us, or was he symbolizing no symbol at all?? I mean, let's focus on the last question. If you were Jesus, or any one of us was Jesus? If you got crucified on a cross, would you want to see a cross on every building to remind you of your own death? Or was it saying that God left his people, meaning black folks. Next I looked at the face on the cover. When I looked at it, it looked sort of like Alkebulan backwards, or what the Greek invaders renamed Africa. Was this saying we should turn back one day and go home? Or could he have been asking black folks why did we turn our back on the birthplace of us all? I may have been over thinking the whole thing, but that's what I did. That is simply the type of person that I was. Two hours passed and I was so deep into this book that if the world ended ilwould've missed it. My phone rung. I looked over.

"**CARLOS!?,**" I yelled out loud. I got scared shitless. I know those crazy movies where the dead person calls and all of a sudden they die. My heart was now beating a mile a minute as I let the phone ring out. After about ten minutes, I calmed down and got back to reading. *"RING!"* It happened again. I let it ring two more times before I looked over at the screen. Carlos named popped up again.

"**WHO THE FUCK IS PLAYING ON A DEAD MANS PHONE?! WHAT KINDA FUCKTARD AND DISRESPECTFUL FUCK DOES THIS?!**" I didn't know if my parents heard me or not, but I really wasn't caring at this point. The phone was eerily silent on the other end.

"**WHO IS THIS?!,**" I yelled again. The cries started to creep through.

"I just call the people in his phone sometimes to try and still bring myself to grips with it all." It was his mom.

"Mrs. Tucker. I so humble apologize. I am so sorry. I never meant to disrespect you. I thought someone was playing on his phone." Her muffled cries were eating at my soul.

"I'm sorry I startled you. That was my baby. My lil stinkbutt. Why did they take him Ramses? Why did they take my baby?" I couldn't even answer her as I sat there and listened to her cry her eyes out. This made me even hate myself even more for dissing my mother when I had the chance to reconcile.

"I shouldn't have to bury my child. Lawd...What do I do Ramses? What do I do?" I couldn't answer. It pained me. I listened to Carlos mom cry her eyes out for the next half hour before she just hung up the phone. I sat in my room down and out. I couldn't even cry. I was done crying months ago when I buried my homey in Oakland. I remember every detail of that day. I flew up with Carlos parents for the funeral with the blessing of my mother. When we arrived, I could sense that magic was about to happen. I hadn't even stepped foot off the plane, but just knowing that I was in Oakland, it felt like I was somewhere where the folks of the city embodied the definition of endurance. The history of this place was filled with blood on the streets from The Black Panthers clashing with everybody who was against the betterment of their people. I was in the place where all hell broke loose when young Oscar Grant was murdered in cold blood by the Amerikkkan UN justice police. Black people had shed so much blood in Oakland that the streets literally talked back to you. We got to baggage claim and were immediately met by some friends of theirs. They damn near forgot about me as they were too busy bonding.

"Oh, I'm sorry," Mrs. Tucker said.

"Julie, this is my adopted son Ramses."

"GIve me a hug then too adopted son." This woman grabbed me tight. So tight that I damn near had the life sucked out of me.

"As she let me go, she introduced me to her husband.

"Ramses huh? Like the great ancestors of ours. Bobby." I shook his hand and damn near had my hand broke from the superman grip he put on it.

"Bobby. Nice to meet you. So what great were you named

after?" I was just making conversation trying to be funny, until the joke was put on me.

"Bobby Seale young man. If you don't know who he was, look him up." I indeed would as by his tone, I could sense a man with a lot of pride in his people. Oh yea, this trip would definitely be a learning experience. We got our bags and immediately headed over to Alameda to a joint called Ole's. It was a small joint where you were damn near on top of the person who you were sitting next too. But when that food came, oh my goodness. I immediately died and went to heaven. I kept it simple with a fat ass stack of pancakes, but it was unlike any you ever tasted. It was like biting into cotton candy. That's how melt in ya mouth them joints was.

We left there and headed towards East Oakland. This city was tough as nails just from the looks of it. I saw the hoards of bruhs out and about walking around, hangin on the corner, all of that. It was crazy. I was 17 and this was the first time I had ever been in any real hood of America. This wasn't Hugo and it damn sure wasn't Newport Beach. Hell, Birmingham even looked like heaven compared to this place. This was life on the other side that I always seen on the news. As bad as I wanted to just get out and walk through these streets, I knew I couldn't. I didn't know how this life operated. And I think that was my biggest strength. I knew my limitations. I knew when and where to make a move. Carlos taught me that when he put me on to playing chess.

"A pawn can move one step at a time. A bishop can move diagonally. But a rook can hit four corners, just like the earth. So who is the most powerful piece?" I remember the day he asked me that.

"The rook." All he did was laugh.

"Nah, the piece you never pay attention too." At that moment in the game, he managed to take my bishop with a knight. He had got me so intrigued in the convo that I lost my entire focus. That was my boy for you. He was a master at throwin' someone off track to keep the pressure off of him. If only he could've kept the pressure off of himself in his own city. A few hours later, we arrived to the house where we were residing at. The funeral was tomorrow. I settled into the basement of this simple three bedroom home. As I plopped on the couch, I noticed a huge box. The grown folks were all upstairs doing whatever, so my intuition kicked in. OLD PHOTOS were written on the side of it. As I started to go through the box, my eyes were opened to a whole new world.

In it were pics of Carlos, his parents, other family members of his, certificates of accomplishment, so on and so forth. It didn't take rocket science to realize that this was his former home. It was almost as if this was pre ordained for me to find. I kept diggin' through the box until I found two things that caught my eye. One was a picture of Carlos and his dad. He had to be about four in the picture, no more than five. Anywho, his dad was cloaked out in all black, with a black glove on, raising it high in the air. Carlos was in his arms, wearing the same ensemble, holding his fist in the air as well. I now see that he merely didn't adopt the lifestyle. He was born into it. Lastly, I found a dusty red book. It was small, with a hard cover. I opened it up and immediately papers started to fall out. I picked up one of the papers and opened it up. It was a letter Carlos wrote to himself in bold marker

Dear Self,

Tomorrow, I leave me to stay the old me in a new body. I leave what I have known for fifteen years. I move into oppression, the life they say we couldn't have. I move to where they ban my people. I promise you, that I will carry the spirit of Huey, Bobby, Eldridge and David and all those who fought so I could stay mentally free. Power to the

people. Black power that is.
Signed, the BLACK man

I folded up the letter and just sat there on my knees crying. The next day, we pulled up to a huge church in a limo. I was honored to have been accepted as family by the Tuckers. I mean, let's face it, Carlos was the closest thing I had to a brother. As I looked out the limo window, I saw a crowd of folks. 'Los was loved in the hood. The numbers didn't lie. I saw one sign that read "He left Oakland, but he never left us." That made me feel special inside to know that one monkey didn't stop no show.

We got out to cheers and all. People around here were happy that Carlos family was back. In a somber moment, you would've thought it was one big party. As we entered the church, I saw it was packed beyond belief. I made it up to the casket and looked at my dude. I couldn't even fathom what I was seeing. I was expecting him to jump up any minute and say

"Nigga what's up?!" It wasn't happening though. My dude was resting for all of eternity. Clad out in his black Ray Guy throwback Raiders Jersey, a Seminary Avenue street sign was nailed in his casket. His dreads were neatly placed on each side of his head, freshly done may I add. As I sat through the hour plus long service, I paid more attention to the people in here than the words being spoken by the preacher. I saw a community. It was something they said didn't exist in the black community. This was false by all means. Even if it took someone dying for everyone to come out, this was community. There was young, old, middle aged, even a few pimps. Coach had sat in the front and gave a great speech about Carlos. He even presented his parents with his framed football and basketball jersey. As we left for the procession to the funeral home, something amazing happened that I never expected. As I got to the limo, Carlos mother got out with a megaphone. I stood outside, wondering what she was about to do.

"Y'all know my son loved the Bay. No matter where we are, the Bay area will always be in our hearts. **SO THIS IS FOR MY SON!!!**" All the windows of the limo and at least fifteen cars behind us lowered.

"**ONE..............TWO..............THREE!!!**" At the same time, the music dropped. I had never seen anything like this. Even the hearse was thumpin. The people who were lining the streets started going crazy and doing the weirdest of dances. I just looked in complete awe. As the words blared through the speakers, I slowly let them sink into my head

"The women like me, I'm dipped in butta I'll rob your brotha pimp the blood out your motha I'm mister stupid doo doo dumb Sumthin Terrible, tell em how we come"

S - T - U - P - I - D
When we go to the club we don't need ID
Everywhere we go its a party yall
We gon get it crackin like the Mardi Gras
Get stupid, Get stupid, Get stupid, Get stupid
Go stupid, Go stupid, Go stupid,
Come and go stupid with me

I truly couldn't believe this. I was back in the limo now, looking at everyone I guess going stupid as we pulled off slowly. Not even three seconds after we got to moving, the police had to stop the precession because folks had come out into the streets dancin'. One dude even jumped on the hood of the hearse and started looking like he was having a convulsion. Then, all the hoods and even the top of the cars had people on 'em. I mean, Times Square on New Year's Eve had nothing on these folks. You would've thought the powers to be had all got taken out and black people were free again.

"A Newport?" I turned my head to see some random cat with dreads had run up to the window.

"Los told me 'bout you on the line. You one of us my nigga." We shared a fist pound and he immediately went to shaking his dreads. All I could do was smile. What I was just told meant the world to me, but my biggest concern was how in the good hell were we gonna get to the cemetery? Actually, I wasn't. I was basking in this moment. The police were trying their damnedest, but it was to no avail. And if they even thought about shooting some unarmed black folks right now, which they were good for, all hell would break loose.

When we finally got to the cemetery, the music had now ceased. As the preacher gave his final words and Los casket was lowered, another round of Bay Area music was played. Man these folks loved their people. More importantly, they truly embodied the concept of laugh at death and cry at birth. All I could do was throw that black rag that he always carried with him in the ground. I would indeed miss that Black Panther attitude. I would miss those golds and random Bay Area slang he used to spit. My dude was truly gone, but in death, I gained even more life. Shit, who knows. Maybe when I came out that tunnel for my first game in college, I might convince the PA guy to have us come out to Thizzle Dance. 'Cause trust, this would probably be the only time I would ever see a party at a cemetery.

The day after the announcement, I took time to relax. I had just a few more months until I had to prepare for college. Even more, I had two more months to prep for graduation. Ever since the season had ended, I had morning workouts running hills and calisthenic drills to prep myself for the college atmosphere. It was even made more difficult wearing an elevation mask, making it feel like I was running at 5,000 feet above sea level. Hell its what I needed to do, seeing that Laramie was over 7,000 feet above sea level. I still was trying to ponder it all and let everything soak in. I was really about to be playing Division 1 ball. Sure, it wasn't at Michigan State, Boise State, Oregon, The great Wolverines of Michigan, but it was division 1 and not everyone could say that. More importantly, not everyone could say they were trying to be a part of a great legacy.

I thought about those 14 players who came before me, paving the way for me to have opportunity. Earl Lee, John Griffin, Willie Hysaw, Don Meadows, Ivie Moore, Tony Gibson, Jerry Berry, Joe Williams, Mel Hamilton, Jim Isaac, Tony Magee, Ted Williams, Lionel Grimes and Ron Hill. Those brothers went through what I could have never probably went through. My struggle was way different than theirs, but one thing we all had in common...we were all black and hated for what we were. As I sat on the rocks after sprinting on the sand, I started to ponder on what I was really about to go through. Life was now about to begin. I came out to Newport with no one to lean on and I was about to head to Wyoming the same way. Except I had eight others this time, and at least 16 other fists would be able to fight with me. I got back to my car after the workout and seen I had a few missed calls from an unknown number. Tired, hungry and just flat out sore, I checked my voicemail. The voice was low, depleted of energy and muffled, so I had to listen to it one more time.

"Brian...I'm almost gone. I...lo....love you. But (cough, cough) if you don't remember anything else, jus....just remember what I tell you is truth. And I know you met Fred. He...he killed your father. Family...fam (cough,cough)... family ain't always family."

I dropped my phone. I didn't wanna believe what I had just heard. I listened to the voicemail about thirty more times. Moms had to be delusional on her deathbed, wherever she was at. I called Fred cause I needed answers.

"What's going on famo?"

"TELL ME IT AIN'T TRUE FRED?! PLEASE TELL ME IT AIN'T!"

"Whoa, whoa, calm down. What's going on?"

"DID YOU KILL MY DAD?! DID YOU FUCKIN' KILL MY DAD?!" He was silent on the other end. **"FRED?!,"** I screamed again. Just then, I heard the most evil laugh.

"Just be lucky I had remorse and didn't kill you little nigga." He hung up the phone and I just sat in my car, gasping for breath and crying. The term a shot to the heart was an understatement right now. I didn't even comprehend where I was at mentally at this point. So much had hit me in such a short amount of time that it was almost too much to bare. I didn't know who to trust anymore. It was like being six years old again. I sped off in the whip from the beach like a loose cannon. Anger, rage and the deepest sense of hurt entered into my soul and I had no regards for anything or anyone. I hit the long stretch of road winding up the hill that led from the strip. I thought my foot hit the brake at one point, but it turned out it was the gas on a sharp turn.

"OH SHIT!," I yelled out. The car spun and I literally blacked out....I woke up on the side of the road, with a woman in my face.

"I called 911. Don't worry. Stay with me." I heard the voice, but I wasn't comprehending what was going on. As my vision cleared, I saw the most beautiful woman I had ever seen.

"Are you good?," she asked me again.

"Re-Renae?"

"Yea, that's me. She smiled. You never called me idiot." She gave me a playful tap on my side to go with those words.

"What happened?," I asked her.

"I was at the light and I seen a car spin. Your back end hit the pole and you just spun two or three more times 'til you came to a complete stop. I was in the car saying oh my God, but when you came stumbling out, I put my blinkers on and hurried over to you. There go the ambulance up the street. You hurt anywhere? You ain't bleeding."

"Naw, I don't feel like I'm hurt. My wrist a bit sore, but I can move it" As she held me in her arms we locked eye contact and I saw something that I never did in my life. That was pure infatuation. The same girl I was so nervous to talk to was right here again.

"So how's this for a first date?" She laughed hysterically as the ambulance came to a stop besides us.

"It's perfect," she responded. The EMT'S got out and immediately tended to me.

"Damn son. The way that car looks in the back, you should be hurt and probably in back pain. Consider yourself lucky." Just then, the other EMT stepped in.

"You're the kid from Newport Harbor going to Wyoming right?"

"Yes sir, that's me."

"Dammit son," as he assisted in helping me.

"I wish you would've went to USC. Is this your girlfriend?" My mind was frozen right now. I looked at him. I looked at her. I looked back at him.

"It's an inadvertent first date sir."

"So you were in the car with him?"

"No, I'm in the car over there with the blinkers on. I just happened to see him and ran out."

"Well," as he sat me up with the other medic. "How is this your first date if y'all don't know each other?"

"Oh we do. He just never called me because he's so shy." The EMT's looked at me as they were wrapping my wrist. At the same time, I saw my parents car coming up the hill.

"Well son. My mama always said God will kick you in the ass if you need it. And obviously, he brought her here again as a kick in the ass to you for not callin'." All that spinning and a big bang resulted in nothing but a wrist contusion. It also resulted in me getting another chance with something that you can only describe in one word...BEAUTIFUL.

10 THE GAME STARTS

"44 dive. 44 dive. **BREAK!!!**" I left the huddle and lined up in the backfield. It was as if everything had slowed down. I looked over towards the sidelines. Renae was sitting out there watching me. The day of my accident, we ended up going out on a date. She couldn't wait to tell me that she had also enrolled at UW. I asked her why. Why would she enroll somewhere like lowly old Laramie, Wyoming? Her answer? Because they had what she wanted, and I was just a bonus.

She had been committed to going there since the beginning of her senior year, so in turn, I was the lucky one. As my mind shifted, I started to think about my adopted parents, who were back in Newport, enjoying the fact that their son was playing big league football. They were gonna be here for our first game against Oregon State. I thought about how they took the chance on a black kid from Oklahoma. I thought about how they fought for me in this imperfect world where everything is literally defined by black and white. I looked down at my jersey. The number nine stood out. To the world, it was just a number. To me, it was the definition of my being. Being black, we have nine lives, much like a cat. One, we are born with two strikes, which already puts us in a bad predicament. Two, between the age of one and five, the world hopes we secretly die young, so we won't make it and they don't have to worry about us growing up. Three, there is the schoolyard blitz of grades K–12. We learned souped up, screwed up and chopped up history that teaches us nothing but hatred and lies. We are taught to buy into a system that was never meant for us to begin with. Fourth, there is the beginning of the new life. Once we are out to fend for ourselves, we learn that our battles haven't even begun. We have not yet seen oppression until we made it to the point that they tried to prevent us from getting to. Fifth, it's the real world scramble. It occurs after the college years. It's when you are trying to establish yourself in the corporate world.

They don't raise us to become business owners. We are raised to be apart of the 95%. The workers, the taxpayers, the laborers. When we enter the workforce, everything has to be on point because we have to impress twice as hard to get our feet wet. Sixth, it's the battle of protecting our next generation. It's no secret that our kids will have it harder than what we had it. It may not be in shackles or chains, gunshots from the police, none of that. But it will be oppression and we have to teach them how to overcome that.

Seventh, it's when we become officially OG's. There was once a Martin episode that stated "Old fools used to be young fools." This is the point where we don't teach the young kid, but the already grown man who may not be grown in his wisdom. Eight, is when we can no longer do for ourselves. In that moment, our ability for doing for others will be shown. Nine, is our death. What will we leave behind? What legacy and knowledge did we pass on? Will folks learn from our death or just look at us as another body laying under a tombstone. I was in my third stage of life and I had better take every opportunity to learn from those in their seventh stage. Lastly, Fred popped in my head. The anger, rage, hatred and despise for a human ran through my blood at this moment.

"Hike!" I took off, following my fullback. As I was met at the three yard line, I kept my legs churning, bouncing off a would be tackler. I headed for the outside where my speed would be an advantage. Everything looked clear. That's until I got smacked from the side.

"WOOOO! Sit ya ass down boy!"

"FUCK OFF ME!," as I pushed Ronald up off of me.

"3rd and goal," said the PA announcer.

"Ram, I got you." That was our backup Willie Turner out of Mississippi. I was pissed. Here it was. My first chance to score at the collegiate level and I blew it. I got to the sideline, coach patting me on the helmet.

"Good job Ram," he said. He might've said good job, but I damn sure didn't believe it. On the next play, Willie ran it in and gave the Brown team the lead. We held on for good after that, winning the brown vs. gold scrimmage 34-28. I was happy for him, but I waited for this moment for so long and didn't deliver. I could only hope that I did better when the season started. Even that would be a challenge because I was the #4 running back on the depth chart. I still had a shot at linebacker, but the defense was pretty much sewed up. I showered up and met Renae outside the stadium.

"Good job babe," as she planted a kiss on my lips. My parents were off in the distance talking to one of my coaches.

"I could've did better. I had a shitty game."

"Babe. It's the scrimmage game. You only got eight carries. Don't worry, you did good." As much as I wanted to be mad, I couldn't. She was here and I never brought the field to our relationship, and vice versa. We walked to the cafe on campus and just enjoyed some food.

"A bruh, you coming to the party tonight?" Nate just appeared outta nowhere it seemed.

"Damn Nate, you ain't gone say hi?"

"Renae, I been knowing you for eons. Let ya man breath for

once in awhile."

"You saying I'm clingy nigga."

"Can you not get ignat round these white folks," he whispered. "I know you Rican and y'all crazy, but girl chill."

"Ok then. Nigga, you saying I'm clingy," she whispered. I just spit my drink out laughing hard at this girl.

"Nate just shook his head. "You chose one, and had to choose the crazy one."

"That's right and she all mine." I planted a kiss on them juicy lips.

"Oh boy," Nate said, rollin his eyes in his head.

"Look. Are you gone be unchained tonight?"

"Yes he will Nate."

"Thank you crazy," as he smiled and walked off. Me and babes finished our meal and headed back to my dorm for some us time before I got it crackin' tonight.

"Open up man!" I heard that loud voice followed by police type knocks. I looked over at the clock and seen it was 9:30 on the dot.

"Ram open the door!" I shot up because I was tired of those loud ass bangs.

"Man what the hell you knockin like you the feds for mane?" Nate had a look on his face like he was disgusted.

"What fool?!," I yelled.

"Look mane, I ain't into that homo shit, so can you throw some clothes on my nigga?" I looked down. I ain't even realize I was ass naked. I guess Renae had threw it on me better than normal. I shut the door, embarrassed as all to be damned, showered up real quick and threw on some clothes. I got outside the dorm room and Nate was long gone. I hit my dude on his cell.

"Where you at mane?"

"I'm downstairs in my whip. C'mon dude." I literally hauled ass downstairs. Soon as I got through the door, there were four white girls walking by.

"Hey ladies. How y'all doin?" I scurried past em, listening to their snickering and one of em saying how she'll tackle me for four quarters and overtime. I let out a chuckle and hopped in the whip. That was gonna be my biggest problem. I had my girl here on campus with me surrounded by all this wild Yellowstone cooch. The black panther was in the land of the snow fox.

"Waddup boy. Where this joint at?"

"Off campus at some house my dude," Nate responded. We rolled into the crispy night, where the air was thinner than a walking stick. My boy kicked on some K. Dot. Good Kidd Maad City was the album to be exact. Wyoming was very different to say the least at nighttime. This city had maybe 31,000 and that's being nice. To say it was big would be lying. To the residents, however, the college made it feel as if it were a big time city.

"Man I gotta get used to this shit bruh," I told Nate.

"HA! Ain't no crazy ass strip on the beach, loud music or half naked women on a daily and you already losin' your mind."

"Not that mane. Just this shit in general."

"Man please. You came from the country to the city. This shit here should be a walk in the park. Oh lemme guess, you ain't got no protection barrier 'round you this time huh?" I looked at him with the side eye.

"Oh don't get mad nigga. It's the truth. Not knockin ya circumstances cause you couldn't control 'em, but the white momma and daddy can't protect you from whitey up here. That's the shit you talking about." As much as I wanted to disagree with him, deep down, he was right. My security blanket was gone. It was me by my lonesome now. I had to prepare myself to handle any and everything that came my way regarding race relations on the solo tip. As we pulled up to the house, I calmed down and was once again at ease. I knew I had a knack of over thinking and it sometimes took my focus away from the task at hand.

Tonight, I just needed to worry about partying and having a good time. Out front, it was your typical party scene. It was August and the summer was winding down here. This would probably be one of the last few parties that involved women wearing short shorts and tank tops. Especially out here in this state where the winter where as cold as polar bear nuts in the Arctic Circle. I was God honest used to these types of women, just not in this setting. I had to play it easy too. I ain't know who knew my girl, if she managed to sneak up in here or what. I wasn't getting in trouble for nobody. That Puerto Rican Culo was too good for me to mess it up.

"Aight mane. Time to go in here and have one of these bitches black snake moan." I could see that Nate and his monstrous built frame were ready for destruction. Hell, he was gonna head to Boise State before this, so white girls were nothing to him. Hell, he even liked them more than sisters. As a matter of fact, he ain't like sisters at all. As long as I had known dude, I never saw him with a sister unless it was his momma or baby sister Courtney. Crazy how he only rocked with white girls, but let Courtney have anyone make a move on her that wasn't black and he was ready to fight. Hell, any man of any race for that matter. He was an overprotective asshole at times. I followed his lead, trying to look as nonchalant as I could possibly be. As we made our way through the crowd in the front, I could already see that a lot of the football team was gonna be up in here. It was like eight of them outside knockin' back beers when we walked up.

"**Sup boi?!**"

"**Sup nigga!,**" Nate said back to Dyron Thomas, our starting quarterback.

"Pharaoh? You sure you can afford to be out? I mean you

got some Puerto Rican ass back on campus and you know niggas round here ain't accustomed to that. So watch 'em." I grabbed the beer as he handed it to me.

"I'm good man. I ain't worried 'bout it. Should I watch out for you though?," I said jokingly. He laughed.

"Nigga please. I grew up in D.C. my nigga. Chocolate City. I ain't fucking with nothing but snow right now. They'll suck you off before class and ride ya shit while you studyin' in the library. Anything with tan skinned is taking a back seat for a while. Ya feel me?" I shook up with my dude. I see he was just as wild as all the other brothers up here.

"Well shit, alright then. Looka here. Y'all gone head, make y'all selves comfortable. Beers in the fridge, cops on our side and ass is all around you. If y'all need me," as two white girls came by his side, grabbin' each arm,

"I might be with them. Ladies. Let's roll" He walked off.

"Do yo' thang man. I'm goin huntin'," Nate said as he took off into the house and left me. I knocked back a little bit of my beer and started making my way through the house. It was the typical college party to say the least. Drunkenness, half naked women, dancing, beer pong, girls kissing girls, so on and so forth. I made my way towards the kitchen to just chill for a hot minute.

"Well, well. You free I see."

"Willie, man. Why y'all sweating a nigga man? She ain't got my in prison."

"I know that," as he took a quick sip of a drink I'd like to call the pink panther.

"I know that, but you better hold that down. Ain't too much ethnicity round these parts. If it's a sister on the basketball team, she probably getting knocked down by a brother from the football team or basketball team. Same with the volleyball players, track girls, all that. You know we need our phat asses. At least I do. I ain't never leaving black. All that sexiness our women got. Mannnnnn. Nigga. And don't let me get a nice chocolate one. I'll hit her lungs and make asthma disappear out her system nigga I'm tellin' you." I spit my drink out laughing at this fool.

"You wild man. So what part of Mississippi you from?"

"Jackson my nigga. Jacktown. Vice Lord. Yessir. But, but my dude. That ain't what it's about anymore. I made it out the hood. Far, far......far away from that muthafucka. I'm a junior in college now. I got turned on to some different shit and I decided to live life. All that gangbangin' shit I used to do, when I look back now, man...that shit wasn't worth it. Nigga I'm fighting another nigga over stars and shit. I get here and it's very few of my kind. That's when I learned that black is powerful. All of us stick together. The niggas from California, niggas from the south, Colorado, Washington, Nebraska, wherever. Hell, ol' Toncho, our strong safety. That nigga from Montana. Born and raised. How many niggas you know from Montana? Here, it's us against everybody. I ain't tryna fight my brother. I'm tryna embrace him. So where you from man? I never got to ask you out there on the field."

"Newport Beach." He took a step back, lookin' me up and down.

"Newport. They got niggas in Newport?"

"Yea man. We everywhere, like you just said." He nodded his head up and down as he took a good swig of that beer in his hand.

"Dude, consider yourself lucky. You had a momma and a father right?"

"Yea."

"Good, good. Least you had a daddy. My old man was a sperm donor. Hit my mom's rolling through Jacktown on a mission one night and that's all she wrote. She gave me the nigga last name and shit, but I ain't seen him since I was seven. But on some real shit, lemme rap this at you. Don't let none of these niggas make you feel bad for growing up rich. I mean, it's crazy. It seems black culture is the only culture who gets offended when one of ours grows up with the quote on quote good life. I mean, I thought that what it was all about. A parent, or parents, making a way so that they kids ain't gotta be raised in the same fucked up environment they was ya feel me." I was intrigued by his words. It was definitely an eye opener to the type of person he was. He didn't need to know about my parents' situation, however. At least not at this time. Right now, it was listening and learning about him time.

"I was just down in your neck of the woods some time back, but in Alabama. I was down there on a project of community enhancement, but it turned into some even wilder shit. Crazy your last name 'cause I was down there with a cat named Fred Turner. He ain't have no kids though." Right then and there, the look in his eyes changed and he dropped his bottle as it shattered on the floor.

"Fred Turner. Fed ass Fred Turner? Nigga......that's the sperm donor who left me." The term it's a small world seemed like it struck my soul and stayed in at that moment as an internal wound.

"Da fuck man?" I watched Willie as he bent over, hands on his knees, shaking his head.

"A man. I'm sorry man. I didn't know."

"Naw man. I'm not mad at you. I'm mad that nigga still alive and don't even care bruh. He a snake in the grass man. He ain't no real man. You know how long I waited of a phone call, or just to see the nigga again? If he was 'round I may not have had to do what I was doin'. Nigga the street niggas raised me. And even some of them niggas had daddies. Even if them muthafuckas was gangstas. Yo, yo I gotta get the fuck up outta here man. I'll holla." Willie took off through the crowded house as I just stood there hating myself for just ruining another man's life. I shouldn't be beating myself up, but if my mouth would've stayed shut, none of this would be happening right now. I had fried more fish in the grease than I had planned. I sat at the party for the rest of the night mingling, but not really getting too much into it. I had once again arrived at a crossroads with another factor. The fatherless child, which wasn't prevalent in the black community like the media would portray, but there was still a major issue with it. I moved out the front of the crib and posted up on Nate's whip 'til he came out at about two in the morning.

"Nigga I been lookin' all over for you. Where you been?"

"I was in the house man. I just got tired and came out here."

"Well shit, how long you been out here?"

"A while," I told him. Nate gave me that look. "Something wrong bruh. I know you. I know you too well," shaking his finger at me.

"But you know what. I don't want any damper news right now because I just got done having a threesome and it's time to bounce. Let's roll and get something to eat fam." We peeled off into the night, heading over to a joint called Shari's for some early morning grub. When we got up in there, half the team was in there getting there smash on. That's if they weren't smashing in the frat house still. As usual, when you get a bunch of college students in one place, early in the morning, it gets loud. Like hella loud. My mind was actually put to ease, however, as I mingled with teammates and enjoyed a fire ass elk omelet, which was something that you could only get here in Wyoming. The night whisked away and everything turned out for the better. After a chill Sunday off, we were back at it again on Monday, studying game film from our first opponent of the year, Oregon State. We were playing them up in Corvallis and it was gonna be a major challenge.

No, they weren't the powerhouse of the Pac 12, but we weren't the big billy bad asses of the Mountain West like Boise State, or TCU when they were in the conference before jumping to the Big 12. It was a huge challenge for us. Bigger schools from bigger conferences scheduled us for what they thought was an easy win. I wanted to change the culture, but I know it would be an uphill battle. Film session was film session and the only thing out of the ordinary was that Willie Turner wasn't here. No one knew where he was at. He didn't pick up his phone, nor was he in his dorm room when one of the players checked in on him.

"Any questions?," coach blurted out as we finished watching how their offense operated. Just then, Willie walked in.

"And where have you been Willie?," coach asked. Willie stayed silent. No response. He walked to the front of the huge 70 inch screen in our facility.

"A coach, can I ask you something?," he said ever so somber.

"Did you ever have a daddy?" We all, including coach looked at him funny.

"Yeah son. Why?"

"So lemme ask you this. Did he leave you?"

"What are you getting at Willie?" With tears in his eyes, he responded with two words.

"This coach." In the blink of an eye, he pulled out a gun and offed himself. We were transfixed. I stood up in utter shock. Coach was frozen stiff, mouth open, splattered in blood. Life had taken a turn that I wasn't prepared for. Teammates swarmed to Willie's side, but I knew it was a wrap. I saw the fragments of his brain splattered across the big screen. I knew it was over. 21 years old. He hadn't even begun to live yet. As pandemonium erupted and chaos ensued, I slowly made my way out of the facility. I got outside and began to ball my eyes out. His death was literally on my hands. I could feel his spirit overtake me in this moment. Once again, I was the lonely kid with no one to run too. It was like being back in Oklahoma. I watched as the ambulance pulled up with some of the team outside waving them down. Suddenly, I felt arms wrap around me.

"You not alone brother. You not alone." It was Nate, reassuring me as I was sprawled out on the concrete crying uncontrollably at this point. I always knew what death felt like, but I never knew what murder felt like...until now. We sat in the visitors' locker room of Oregon State almost two weeks to the day that Willie took his own life. We had the number 24 decals on the back of our helmets. As I was getting my ankles wrapped up in the training room, I thought about all those times I looked at the news when they talked about soldiers coming back from the war with post traumatic stress disorder. I would never know what it would be like to have a million bullets fired at me at once, in 140 degree heat, with tactical gear on. I could, however, try and understand it.

Mental illness was a serious issue in this country and we had to take a second look at it. I'm not talkin' about mass shootings, as a lot of times, they are just committed by people who have no regards for life or they're set up by some people of a higher authority. I'm talking about the serious person who can't sleep at night due to war. The person who begs for help, but is constantly ignored because everyone just blows them off as crazy. The kid who was born mentally challenged that I tripped up back in the days because he was different. It's not a game. Willie was suffering once he found out the man who abandoned him was alive and breathing. I didn't follow up on him to see how he was. I could have maybe prevented what happened. At the end of the day, however, the Good Lord has a method to his madness. I wasn't the one to condemn Willie to heaven or hell. If anything, I had to condemn myself for not helping. Sometimes, the loudest cry for help comes from the mouth that is closed shut.

"All done Pharaoh. Go get em."

"Thanks Dan." Dan was our trainer and strength coach. I walked back to the locker area and threw on my shoulder pads and jersey. It felt different. It felt good. My dream was no longer a dream. I was now living. I took it over to the mirror. I looked myself in the eyes. That Wyoming across my chest with the number 9 made a statement. I was here. This was my moment. My time had come. The specialty players had begun to file out onto the field. I didn't make it past number three on the depth chart, but coach was using me on special teams as a kick returner. As I got to the tunnel, he stopped me.

"Ramses," as he put his hand on my shoulder.

"Yes coach?" Tell me what do you think when you look out of this tunnel?" I looked out into Reser Stadium and I looked hard. I saw nothing but black and orange. A lot of the orange was empty seats, but I knew that would all change real soon.

"I don't know coach. I don't know what I am supposed to see."

"Look, I know you haven't been yourself since Willie died. I see it in your eyes. Just know that I watched my old man drink himself to death after my mother died. He didn't talk to God anymore after she passed. I know what it's like to lose someone close. So today, when you get in this game, win or lose, you put your damn best effort in there. You carry the burden and pain that you have filled up in your soul right now and you release it in a positive way. You're made for this. You have people watching you and you don't even know it." He patted my helmet and walked off. I just stood there for about ten seconds, telling myself that I was ready for this and that I was meant for this moment. I walked out the tunnel and was just in awe. Looking at 45,674 seats that were half full was a site to indeed see. College football was here and there was no turning back at this point. Warm ups finished and we headed back to the locker room to unwind before it was time to kickoff.

"How you feel?," Big Darcell asked me.

"It damn sure ain't high school no mo' man."

"Yea, that's for damn sure," he responded. We then sat there, nervous as all get out. You could tell we were freshmen. All the older, more experienced players were cool, calm and collective. Then coach entered the room.

"GATHER 'ROUND! TAKE A KNEE!," he yelled. Then, I heard a speech like no other I had ever heard before in my life.

"THAT'S IT. GET YOUR OWN FOCUS. THERE ISN'T ALWAYS SOMEONE AROUND TO GIVE YOU MOTIVATING WORDS! IN LIFE, THERE ISN'T ALWAYS SOMEONE THERE TO BOOST YOU UP! IN LIFE......THERE ISN'T ALWAYS SOMEONE THERE TO SAVE YOU! THINK ABOUT 24 AND BOOST YOURSELVES! BE IN THE TUNNEL! FIVE MINUTES!" He walked out and left us all there to ponder those words. The locker room was quiet. We all looked at each other. No words, just looking. That's when Dyron got up.

"FOR NUMBER 24! LET'S GET IT!" We erupted with a passion and literally ran to the tunnel. We were Wyoming. Win or lose, we were gonna leave our hearts on this field. Not just for our fallen brother, but because we were men. As we got to the base of the tunnel, my focus was sharper than an owl that spotted a jackrabbit form a mile away. It was just like when I was at the University of Oregon. I saw nothing but the end zone and a full stadium that awaited my arrival.

"Ramses!" I heard people calling my name.

"Yo Ram!" It was amazing to take in the crowd waiting for me.

"Ramses. A nigga?" It was Ronald Clark tappin' me on the shoulder.

"A some white boy callin' your name right there like crazy." I was so zoned out that I thought it was an illusion. I looked up towards the stands.

"TEP! SUP BOI!" He gave me the thumbs up right as we were introduced. I was on cloud nine as I sprinted out with my team. The course of boos out did the small section of gold that was cheering for us, but I truly didn't care. My mans was here watching me on the biggest stage that I would probably ever be on. The term adrenaline rush was an understatement.

"RAMSES!" I looked back at coach as we were about to take the field.

"REMEMBER WHAT I TOLD YOU!" I nodded my head to agree and headed down to the five yard line. They deferred, so the pressure was put on me from jump. My heart was racing a mile a minute. This was it I thought. You always saw return guys on TV pacing up and down their area of the field. I always thought they were trying to stay loose. In some cases, that may be true. However, for me, I was secretly pleading to God that my blockers stayed in front of me so I wouldn't get smacked. This was college and everyone was big. Everyone was fast. Everyone more than likely had dreams of making it to the NFL, so their main goal was to bring the boom.

I seen the kicker off in the distance raise his hand and look to both sides of him. That was the international football signal that he was about to lay a boot. The crowd noise built up all the way until he kicked the ball. *BOOM!* A loud cannon of some sorts went off and my eyes went to the air. There was no way in hell I was bringing this one back as I was almost seven yards deep in the end zone when I caught it. As I tossed the ball to the ref and ran back to the sideline, I saw coach signaling for me to stay in. What the hell, I thought. I wasn't ready for this. This man was trying to get me killed on the first game of the season.

"You ready fresh meat?," Dyron asked me in the huddle.

"Let's go man," I said, trying to sound as confident as I could ever be.

"Aight now. Let's open the flood gates on the first play. Play action Cowboy swing. They got one safety over the middle. Easy pickings. Ready.....**BREAK!!!**" I went out to the slot on the weak side of the field. I saw their defense. One deep safety. A linebacker split between me and the tackle. I thought it would be easy pickings like Dyron said. Suddenly, they switched up, checking into a 5-2-4 look.

"**CHECK, CHECK LEAD, CHECK LEAD!,**" Dyron yelled. I shifted back into the backfield, solo, just me. I knew the rock was coming to me. No fullback on my first division 1 play right? Fuck my life if everyone comes on a blitz, I thought.

"**HUT!**" I took that first step towards the left side, got the handoff and seen daylight. Right off my left side guard, I ripped through the three hole, cut back right on a defender, making him miss and trucked their safety downhill for a 14 yard gain. I got up thinkin' my shit didn't stink.

"Good shit man," said Big E-Dubb, a big country boy O lineman from Cody, Wyoming who was an all state selection three years ago in high school and the reigning Mountain West offensive lineman of the year.

"**RAM!**" I turned around to see I was being pulled out by Josh Lehto, our original starter at tailback. I hauled it off to the sidelines next to coach.

"Good job dammit," he said.

"You're the future of this team." I stood there, Gatorade squirt bottle in hand, soaking in those six words that he had just told me. I had arrived. The black kid had departed while the black man had touched down. I looked down at the

number nine on my chest. I placed my hand over it.
"That was for you Carlos," I whispered to myself.

ABOUT THE AUTHOR

It's amazing what can happen when pen meets a paper. The ideas that are brought forth by the author can turn a simple thought into a masterpiece. How did Joe McClain get into writing??? That's a great question to ask. Living in Guam back in 2013, he took interest in a short story contest that was originated by Brianni Blue, a well known spoken word artist out of Oakland, CA, who appeared on TV One's "Versus and Flow." Poetry was always easy, but to write a full length story??? That was a different ball game and one Joe had no idea how to comprehend.

"My biggest thing was simply what to write about. I would literally sit in front of my computer for an hour and not type anything," he says. After much debate, he turned on some old Dipset and the rest was history.

"JR Writer was spitting a verse on one track, and immediately I came up with the title of THE WRITERS BLOCK. From there, I began to write about my life and add some thrill to my story for entertainment purposes." In a span of 30 days, Joe had finished his first story, and added another notch to his resume. Fast Forward to February 2014. He had now returned stateside to California. During a visit to the Lyrical Exchange open mic in San Diego, a longtime friend, DJ Redlite, put him in contact with Caujuan Mayo, a friend of his who also ran his own publishing company.

"I wasn't even thinking about getting the story published. I honestly did it to pass the time by while I was living over there, and because I thought it would be something cool to do." After contacting Caujuan and arranging a meeting with him, the two immediately hit it off and began to talk business. Two weeks later, after careful analysis of this new situation, Joe signed on the dotted line for "THE WRITERS BLOCK" to be published. On August 4th, 2014, "THE WRITERS BLOCK" was released and took off to be a hit in the short story genre.

"I honestly didn't know what to expect. When I seen and read the reviews people were leaving me on Amazon, I know I had indeed did something special." To this date, "THE WRITERS BLOCK" has sold over 1,000 copies and continues to sell. With this project under his belt, Joe released his second book entitled "BANDAGES" in March of 2015.

"It's a well thought out story," he says. "This isn't Writer's Block. With that book, I put together something and didn't think to much of it. After seeing how well people received it, I really studied the process of writing and putting collective thoughts into a great story that people could really relate to. If I'm not upgrading, then I'm downgrading."

How this young man transitioned into an unknown arena and made it work for him is beyond amazing. As a product of the inner city, he is really transcending the art of writing by opening people up to a world that many have not experienced. Television can only give you a glimpse. To make a person feel like they are actually there, that is something completely different. Joe McClain Jr. is definitely on the way to becoming a top tier author and more importantly, an excellent figure in the black community who shows that anything is indeed possible. He has many more book projects planned to include "The Square Rt of Pain" and "BANDAGES 2: Wounds Re-opened."

What is forthcoming for this great author is beyond amazing. If the world does not know who he is, they will certainly know very soon.

IF YOU ENJOYED READING
"A BLACK MAN HAS NINE LIVES"
PLEASE LEAVE A REVIEW ON AMAZON.COM
http://ow.ly/JggvZ

ALSO AVAILABLE

When his father passed at 12, Mr. Terrelle Washington grew up fast and survived the dangerous streets of East Chicago, Indiana. After finding out his deceased father left him a large inheritance, he decided to leave for California and achieve his dream of becoming a published Author. However, the land of Hollywood stars was soon transformed into a maze of unforeseen obstacles he never expected on his way to the top. How will it play out??? Will he achieve his dream, or will it be shattered into a nightmare of failure.

A hard life in the inner city. Made it through. About to prepare for the next step of most young men. College. That was all until one fateful night to where freedom was taken away. Now, in the battle of his young life, a young man has two options. Die in prison, or snitch and possibly get another chance. Either choice will draw consequences, but what will he choose??? What wounds will be healed, and what wounds will be re-opened???

Ricky Walters grew up in the gritty streets of San Diego California. Upon quitting his security job, he meets an ex pimp name Trust who teaches him everything about the pimp game. Ricky ends up turning out a young Asian girl name Yuki, changes his name to Jackpot, and jumps knee deep in the pimp game. Jackpot makes a conscious decision to become the biggest pimp to ever play the game and goes cross country. Here, is where Jackpot finds himself getting money, ducking the police, feuding with haters, vindictive females, snitches, and eventually doing time in the penitentiary.

Let Me Pimp Or Let Me Die 2, tells the story of a few female workers in the "Game," told through their lives as you see and find out what motivates a woman to start ho'n and sell her body. Re-visit some of your favorite characters from part 1 and see what drove them into the lifestyle that they chose. Each story different but ultimately the same.

Graphic and not for the faint of heart, the scenes take place in a realistic setting with many twist n turns you won't see coming. Find out how F.A.B Killed Sunshine and what happened in those last moments. How Green Eyes got hooked on drugs and the real reason she left Jackpot for dead in prison. Or the number one question...Will Jackpot Return To The Game?

Xavier Sands and Danielle Seville meet at the grand opening of Xavier's nightclub, and it happens to be his birthday. Not to be left out, Danielle is celebrating her birthday as well. As the two grow closer, wedges are driven between them behind the scenes, by their own mothers!

Xavier and Danielle both work for King Kole Konners, in different venues, but when the King is shot, all bets are off. The kingdom having just survived the Chase St. John mutiny in South Nubia, is rocked once again. The assassin begins picking off the King's top people, leading to Danielle being kidnapped.

Xavier vows vengeance on the person, or persons responsible for the shooting of the King. During her kidnapping ordeal, Danielle learns a horrible, life changing secret. Just as her world is rocked, Xavier learns the same shocking truth from his mother.

"Freeze mother fucker!" a cop spat, but the Skyline hardhead wasn't trying to hear it. He blindly reached on the floor for his gun as he slowly regained his eyesight. Jail wasn't an option for the young rida. He knew he had done too much to turn back. Fuck it, he was gonna hold court in the streets. As he placed his hand on the gun that laid dormant on the floor, that would be as close as he got to picking it up and letting off a shot...

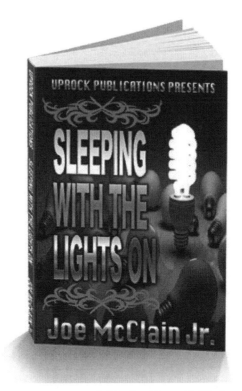

Lamar Atteley III has made out a good life for himself. He has turned Las Vegas into his own personal playground after surviving the rough environment of Detroit, Michigan. However, with a new job offer, he now has to prepare for a new chapter of his life that will either make or break him. His adventure will take him to the other side of the world......to Guam. Now, he will be tested harder than any other point in his life. With all new surroundings, more money, women at his disposal and a different breed of people in general, the question is can he handle it all. When its all said and done, you will understand why we sometimes sleep with the lights on.

Wake n Bake the natural way. Weed consumption through digestion is a lot healthier than smoking it, which is why we put together this book of tasty meals with a 420 kick to keep you happy, smiling and feeling good! From breakfast, lunch, dinner to dessert we got you covered. Enjoy some weed laced french toast for breakfast. Craving a light snack? Try some of our weed hummus. End the night with a homemade weed pizza and cheesecake for dessert. We even have a recipe for cooking oil and weed butter. Over 30 different recipes to choose from. Meals so quick and easy to make, you'll wonder why you didn't pick up this book sooner. Simple everyday recipes made easy will have you feeling like a pro in the kitchen! No more having to buy overpriced edibles from the dispensary . Now you can make all those delicious treats yourself.

COMING SOON
P.E.E.R.S
By: Joe Mac

UPROCK AUDIO BOOKS

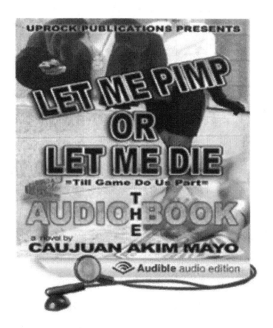

Don't have the time to read? Well, we have the solution. Pick up your audio version of "Let Me Pimp Or Let Me Die." The book by Caujuan Akim Mayo that started it all. Listen to this action pack audio book, loaded with special sound effects and cinematic music for dramatic effect, like no other audio book you've ever heard before. This is the audio book, that changed the game and set the bar.

Website: www.uprockpublications.com
Emails: uprockp@gmail.com
Facebook: uprockpublications
Twitter: uprockpub
Contact: (619) 259-0298

Made in the USA
San Bernardino, CA
12 April 2018